epicure

chocolate

Copyright © 2006 John Fairfax Publications Pty Ltd.
201 Sussex Street, Sydney, NSW, 2001

Editor Kylie Walker
Art director Ian Warnecke
Photography Marina Oliphant
Cover and recipe styling Caroline Velik
Cover photography Marina Oliphant
Portrait photography Simon Schluter, Rebecca Hallas, Melanie Faith Dove, Marina Oliphant
Proofreading Patrick Witton
Pre-press The Age Imaging Centre. Gaynor Rumble, Peter Keane, Richard Wilson

Acknowledgments: Wooden laminate backgrounds supplied by Designer Laminates. Jasper Conran glassware (tiramisu and cocktail) from Minimax. Chocolate curls page 6 by Cacao. All other props stylist's own. Photographs on pages 34, 103 and 144 taken on location at Melbourne Supper Club, 161 Spring Street, Melbourne 3000, (03) 9654 6300.

Managing Editor, Fairfax Books: Michael Johnston (02) 9282 2375
Senior Product Manager, Fairfax Enterprises: Linda MacLennan (02) 9282 3054
Publishing Manager, Fairfax Enterprises: Stephen Berry (03) 9601 2232
General Manager, Fairfax Enterprises: Lauren Callister (02) 9282 3904
General Manager, Fairfax Strategy and Enterprises: Ben Way (02) 9282 1677

For copyright or contributor questions please contact Linda MacLennan

Printed in Australia by McPherson's Printing Group

ISBN: 192 119 030 2

epicure

chocolate

recipes from 20 years of indulgent ideas

contents

A dark mistress or a comforting friend. Bitter or sweet – or even savoury. A simple pleasure or a decadent indulgence. Is there an ingredient with more guises than chocolate?

In the pages that follow, we celebrate many of them. We are also celebrating the 20th birthday of *The Age's* weekly food and wine section, Epicure.

For two decades, Epicure has set out to inform, entertain and inspire. Tuesday March 11, 1986 saw the publication of the first stand-alone edition. It was an eight-page broadsheet, published in black and white. Over the years that followed, it gained colour and changed size. Epicure critics sipped, spat, chewed and savoured endless wines and meals. Our writers tackled everything from Fair Trade to where to buy fish. Epicure garnered awards, provoked discussion and gathered a loyal readership. And within its pages, we shared thousands of recipes.

In that first edition, the word "chocolate" appeared 15 times. And, of course, there was a chocolate recipe – a mousse – shared by columnist Beverley Sutherland Smith.

Over the years that followed more than 300 chocolate recipes were published in the pages of Epicure. They reflected the changing tastes of the times: a chocolate pecan pie in 1986, strawberry chocolate cups in 1988 and various mud cakes in the 1990s. Brownies first appeared in 1989 and have remained an enduring favourite to this day.

There were lean years – only four recipes containing chocolate appeared in 1991 – and times of plenty. In 1993, editor Rita Erlich started, "as a whimsy", a column called My Favourite Chocolate Cake. "Everyone loves chocolate cake, I thought ... let's ask a few people for their favourite versions." A chocolate storm followed. Recipes (and chocolate cakes) flooded into the Epicure office. Readers held baking parties to compare recipes; some faithfully grabbed bowl and spoon each week, baking every single recipe that appeared in the column, which ran for more than a year. The series gave birth to a book, edited by Rita and published in 1995, called *50 Fabulous Chocolate Cakes*.

And now we have a book devoted to chocolate in all its guises, from biscuits to brownies, cakes to confectionery, even a few savoury recipes.

Many of the great chocolate recipes published in Epicure came from the food writers and chefs who have been part of the Epicure team over the years – Beverley Sutherland Smith was followed as cooking columnist by Jill Dupleix, Donna Hay, Luke Mangan, Stephanie Alexander and Brigitte Hafner. All are represented in this book.

Over the years, local chefs and cooks, visiting international stars, *Age* journalists and many others have also shared their favourite recipes and some of those appear here, too. Many of the editors who have guided the section – Peter Weiniger (1986-88), Janne Apelgren (1988-89), Gayle Austen (1989-91), Richard Yallop (1991), Rita Erlich (1992-94), Roslyn Grundy (1994-96), Stephanie Wood (1997-2000) and John Lethlean (2000-01) – have also contributed.

Finally, we asked our readers to share their favourite recipes. Almost 200 recipes filled the mailbox. Some were simple, some grand. Some were recent creations, others handed down through many generations.

The stories that came with some recipes evoked an aching wonder. Readers shared stories of finding recipes believed lost after the death of a parent and rediscovered in a handwritten notebook. One told of how cooking a particular recipe was a way of sharing something of her mother with the grandchildren she never knew; another reader wrote of the strength of spirit shown by his mother, who at the age of 18 was left to hold together, with the help of aunts and uncles, a family of six siblings after the deaths of her parents.

Other tales illustrated the way recipes slide and shift along the bonds of friendship, strengthening them as they go. Many readers shared their version of a recipe given to them by a friend. From others came the recipes they make for their friends – the deeply indulgent, alcohol-laced wedding cakes, the birthday cakes, the biscuits baked for when friends drop by.

We were overwhelmed by the willingness of our readers to share their recipes. We hope you, the readers of this book, enjoy this collection, too.

Kylie Walker, Epicure editor

biscuits, brownies + slices 011

Macadamia and white chocolate brownies

A delicious, cakier-style brownie studded with nuts and chocolate. Cook for 20 minutes for what Natali describes as "the yummiest, gooiest brownie ever", or for an extra 5 minutes if you like a firmer texture.

300g dark chocolate, chopped

115g unsalted butter, chopped

150g castor sugar

2 eggs, beaten

1 cup plain flour

180g white chocolate, chopped

100g unsalted macadamias, chopped

Preheat oven to 180C. Line a 20cm square tin with nonstick baking paper.

Place dark chocolate, butter and sugar in a stainless-steel bowl over a pan of simmering water. Stir until ingredients have melted.

Remove from heat and leave to cool for 5-10 minutes. Stir in the beaten eggs. Mix in the flour, then stir in the white chocolate and macadamias until well combined.

Spoon into prepared tin. Bake for 20-25 minutes.

Remove and cool before cutting into pieces.

Reader Natali Pride

Crisp cocoa cookies with chocolate chips

"This very rich, dark chocolate treat is an old favourite in our house. The recipe is for so many because I think if you are going to go to the trouble of baking, you may as well do a lot. Besides, a dozen − or two − always disappear from the cooling rack."

250g unsalted butter, softened
1 cup castor sugar
½ cup dark brown sugar
2 eggs
½ tsp vanilla essence
2 cups plain flour
1 tsp baking soda
4 tbsp Dutch cocoa
250g dark chocolate chips

Preheat oven to 190 C.
   Cream the butter and castor sugar. Mix in the brown sugar.
   Add eggs one at a time and mix well. Add the vanilla.
   Sift the flour, baking soda and cocoa into the bowl and mix well.
   Add the chocolate chips (keep some in reserve to add to that last bit of mixture that would otherwise go without).
   Scoop teaspoons of the mixture onto a baking tray covered with baking paper, leaving room for the biscuits to spread. (For larger biscuits, use a tablespoon.)
   Bake for 10-12 minutes.
Makes 5 dozen small cookies (or about 30 larger cookies)

Reader Elizabeth Banfield

New York special

"Making this slice brings back wonderful childhood memories. I was a member of our church's girls group and one of our leaders was a wonderful American lady, who would from time to time make this slice. Eventually, my mother asked her for the recipe. It is extremely rich, so my mother would only make it for special occasions – and to this day I still make it only occasionally as I can't stop at one piece. The only change I make to the recipe is to sometimes make a double quantity of the second layer – so I don't waste the second half of the pudding mixture and because that layer is so yummy, it can never be too thick!"

First Layer

110g margarine
½ cup sugar
3 tbsp cocoa
2 cups biscuit crumbs
⅔ cup desiccated coconut
⅓ cup walnut crumbs
⅓ cup crushed nuts
1 egg
1 tsp vanilla essence

Second layer

50g margarine
1½ cups of icing sugar
½ packet of vanilla-flavoured instant
   pudding mixture (dry).
milk

Third layer

80g cooking chocolate
1 tbsp of butter

Grease a 22cm square tin.
For the first layer, melt margarine and mix in the sugar and cocoa. Set aside. Mix together biscuit crumbs, coconut and nuts. Mix into this the egg and vanilla and then mix in the sugar/cocoa/margarine mixture.

Press into the tin and place in fridge.

For the second layer, melt margarine and mix with icing sugar and pudding mixture.

Add enough milk to make this spreadable onto the first layer. Return slice to fridge.

For the third layer, melt chocolate and butter over hot water and spread over the second layer.

Allow to set, then cut into 2.5cm squares. Keep in fridge.

Variation: An alternative for the third layer is to melt 85g of copha with 60g of drinking chocolate.

Reader Glynis Smalley

Big flat fudgy chippers

Dried strawberries (you'll find them amongst the other dried fruits in most supermarkets) are intensely sweet. Throw them, and a good portion of white choc chips, into a fudgy, buttery dough and the result is a big, flat, super-rich biscuit. Don't worry if yours don't look like the ones in the picture. How much these spread can vary quite a lot depending on the type of tray you use and what shelf you cook the biscuits on. (This dough freezes well, too, so you can cook half the mix and put the rest away to bake later.)

100g white chocolate bits (weighed and placed in
   the fridge – particularly important if working
   in a hot climate or hot kitchen)
100g dark chocolate melts
100g salt-reduced butter, at room temperature
100g light muscavado sugar
115g castor sugar
1 small egg
½ tsp vanilla essence
140g plain flour, sifted
45g dried strawberries, sliced into 2-3mm
   wide strips

Preheat oven to 180C. Make sure racks are in the top half of the oven. Line each of two trays with a double layer of baking paper.

Melt dark chocolate in microwave or double boiler. Set aside.

Use electric beater to cream butter with sugars until pale and smooth. Add egg and vanilla and beat well. Add sifted flour and melted chocolate.

Finally stir in, by hand using a large spoon, the dried strawberry strips and the white chocolate.

Scoop up rough balls of mixture (a bit bigger than the size of a whole walnut) and place well apart on trays – they spread a lot. (If freezing, put the balls of dough, spaced apart so they don't touch, on a layer of baking paper in a flat-based air-tight container and place into freezer.

Once frozen, they can be moved into a sealable bag or a smaller container.)

Place trays into oven. After 5 minutes, swap trays between racks, rotating them as you do so (most ovens have hot spots). Cook another 5-6 minutes. Remove from oven. (For that really rich, fudgy texture, these biscuits need to come out when they look like they might need another minute. But some people tell me they like the slightly drier style of the ones I call overcooked – try them both ways and make up your own mind!)

Allow to cool on trays for at least 10 minutes before moving to cooling racks.

Cook remaining dough as above.
Makes about 25 8-9cm biscuits

Kylie Walker, Epicure editor

Brammeringues

"These bite-sized meringues – inspired by a Stephanie Alexander recipe – are good on their own and fantastic with berries and cream or ice-cream," says Eliza Bram of her recipe. Indeed, they are fantastic either way – unexpected little bits of chocolate buried in a lightly chewy meringue. Serve them as a biscuit or as a dessert.

6 egg whites
200g castor sugar
175g dates, stoned and chopped
150g raw almonds, chopped
175g dark chocolate (use the best you can afford), chopped

Preheat oven to 150C and line two baking trays with baking paper.

Beat egg whites until just stiff, then slowly beat in sugar. Fold in dates, nuts and chocolate. Spoon onto the trays and cook for about 20 minutes (this time depends a lot on your oven and the baking trays you use). Cook a little longer for a completely crunchy meringue or a bit less for a crisp outside and gooey inside.

Turn off the oven and leave the door ajar until completely cool. Store in airtight containers.
Makes 60

Reader Eliza Bram

Chocolate-coated rum raisin cookies

Donna Hay is best known to many Australian – and increasingly, international – food lovers through the award-winning magazine that bears her name. But before she began that adventure, she shared many wonderful recipes during her time as Epicure's weekly food columnist, including these delicious choc-top cookies.

125g butter, softened
¼ cup rum
1 cup brown sugar
1 egg
2 cups plain flour
1 tsp baking powder
¾ cup raisins
250g dark or milk chocolate, melted

Preheat oven to 180C.

Place the butter, rum, sugar, egg, flour and baking powder into a food processor and process until well combined. Place mixture into a bowl and stir through the raisins.

Place spoonfuls onto lined baking trays and bake for 12-15 minutes or until just golden. Cool on wire racks.

When the cookies are cold, dip them into melted chocolate and allow to set on wire racks.
Makes 24

Food writer Donna Hay, 2001

Cornflake crunchies

"These have been in my recipe book forever," says Dorothy Bransgrove. "I am 84 years young but still enjoy making my favourite bikkies to enjoy with friends when they call in." Leave the cornflakes whole for a crunchier, crumbly-textured biscuit, or crush them lightly for a smoother texture. We suggest using low-salt butter, to balance the high levels of salt found in most brands of cornflakes.

175g butter, preferably reduced salt or unsalted
2 tsp cocoa
50g sugar
175g self-raising flour
50g cornflakes
1 cup chocolate icing (use your own recipe, or see page 178)
30 walnut halves

Preheat oven to 150C.

Slightly melt the butter (e.g. soften in microwave – it doesn't need to be completely liquefied), add the cocoa and sugar and beat well with an electric beater. Add flour gradually, mixing between additions, and lastly the cornflakes.

Space small spoonfuls of dough on a greased tray then flatten with a wet knife. Bake for 15 minutes. Leave on tray to cool, then put a dab of chocolate icing on each one and place a walnut half on top.
Makes about 30

Reader Dorothy Bransgrove

Candy cane cookies

"As far as my children are concerned, there's only one thing better than chocolate chip cookies, and that's the chocolate chip cookies I make at Christmas, studded with candy canes. I've adapted an excellent recipe from *Family Circle Basics to Brilliance Biscuits Recipes* (Murdoch Books, 1996) for these biscuits, which need to be watched in the last few minutes. They must be cooked just long enough for the candy canes to melt and the cookies to crisp, but not so long that the candy oozes out."

150g unsalted butter
¼ cup soft brown sugar
⅓ cup castor sugar
1 egg yolk
1 tsp vanilla essence
½ tsp peppermint essence
1½ cups self-raising flour, sifted
½ cup dark choc chips
½ cup milk choc chips
2-3 roughly chopped peppermint candy canes

Preheat oven to 180C. Spray two biscuit trays with cooking oil and line with nonstick baking paper.

Using electric beaters, beat the butter, sugars and yolk until light and creamy. Add the vanilla and peppermint and beat to combine. Add the flour and mix to form a soft dough. Remove bowl from the mixer and stir in half the chocolate chips and the chopped candy canes until combined.

Roll one level tablespoon of the mixture at a time into balls. Press the remaining chocolate bits firmly onto the tops of the balls. Arrange the balls on the prepared trays, allowing room for spreading. Bake for 10-12 minutes, or just until the candy begins to melt (but not liquefy) and the cookies become golden. Allow the cookies to cool on the trays before you lift them off.
Makes about 24

Roslyn Grundy, Epicure editor 1994-96

This recipe appears with the permission of Murdoch Books.

Chocolate almond shortbread

"This is a classic shortbread with a twist. I adore the combination of almonds and chocolate, so added both. I also use a cutter and make small thin biscuits, rather than fatter shortbread fingers. The biscuits have that lovely sandy shortbread texture and a delicious flavour. A couple of things to note. The butter must be at room temperature. Use your hands to mix it all − it's the best way of knowing when everything is well amalgamated. The other thing is that the almonds should be ground in a blender − a food processor doesn't get them fine enough. The chocolate should be finely grated, too."

130g lightly salted butter
100g plain flour
60g ground rice
60g castor sugar
25g almonds, finely ground
45g dark chocolate, finely grated

Preheat oven to 180C.

Put the butter into a bowl. Sift the flour, ground rice and sugar over the butter, add the ground almonds, and mix until it is nearly like pastry. Add the chocolate, and mix until well incorporated into the dough.

Put onto a floured board and pat out with your hands, gently (it should be about 3-5mm thick). Cut with a biscuit cutter − I like a heart-shaped cutter − and place onto greased baking trays. Any scraps can be amalgamated, then patted out again so more shapes can be cut. Chill the trays of biscuits (for about an hour) before cooking.

Bake for about 25 minutes, until browned but not burnt. Don't overcook them. Because of the chocolate, the biscuits are much darker than conventional shortbread.

Remove carefully to a cooling rack.
Makes about 40 hearts

Rita Erlich, writer, author and Epicure editor 1992-94

Viennese brownies

The almonds on top provide a lovely textural contrast with the soft, moist, cakey brownie layers and the thick, smooth cheesecake layer in the middle. Simply devine. Marie has been making this recipe for 40 years, after coming across it in America, in an advertisement for Philadelphia cream cheese.

60g unsweetened chocolate (see note below)
½ cup margarine
2 eggs
1 cup sugar
¾ cup plain flour
½ tsp baking powder
½ tsp salt
sliced almonds

Filling

250g Philadelphia cream cheese, at room temperature
⅓ cup sugar
1 egg
¼ tsp almond essence

Preheat oven to 180C.

To make the filling, combine softened cream cheese, sugar, egg and almond essence.

For the batter, melt chocolate and margarine together; cool. Beat eggs, add sugar and chocolate mixture. Sift together flour, baking powder and salt, add to chocolate mixture and mix well. Pour half of chocolate batter into a greased 20cm square pan; spread with cream cheese mixture. Top with remaining batter. Sprinkle with almonds.

Bake for about 45 minutes. Cool in tin.

Note: Unsweetened chocolate can be hard to find in Australia. The recipe will also work well with a good quality, high-cocoa-percentage (65-75 per cent) chocolate.

Reader Marie Buchanan

This recipe is Copyright of Kraft Foods. Philadelphia is a trademark of Kraft Foods.

Sam's hedgehog

"Everyone should have a hedgehog in their repertoire," says Sam Douros. We agree. Sam's version is one for nut-lovers − chunky, nut-studded slices with a rich chocolate topping.

2 x 250g packets sweet plain biscuits
1 cup walnuts
300g butter
¾ cup Dutch cocoa
1¼ cups castor sugar
3 eggs
Icing
250g good dark chocolate
2 tbsp canola oil

Put biscuits and nuts in a food processor and whiz until roughly chopped (or put them in a freezer bag and crush the living suitcase out of them).

Melt the butter, then add the sugar and cocoa and stir until the sugar is dissolved.

Remove from the heat and when cooled a little (i.e. warm, not hot) beat the eggs into the mix with a whisk or an electric wand until thick and glossy.

Mix in the nut mixture and press into a lamington tin (about 19cm x 30cm). Cover and refrigerate.

Make the icing by melting the chocolate and oil in a saucepan on very low heat and then pour on top of the cooled hedgehog. Tap the tray on the bench to get all the air bubbles out.

Refrigerate again until set and then cut into fingers or squares.

Reader Sam Douros

Herbie's hedgehog

Like brownies, hedgehogs come in many guises. "I created this recipe about 20 years ago to satisfy my husband's search for the 'perfect hedgehog'," says Kerry Herbison. "It's a quick, easy everyday recipe for those who love to indulge every day."

2 x 250g packets Marie biscuits
250g butter
2 cups sifted icing sugar
4 tbsp cocoa
6 tbsp desiccated coconut
2 eggs, beaten
Icing
2 cups sifted icing sugar
2 tbsp cocoa
½ tbsp butter, melted
4 tbsp hot water
2 tbsp desiccated coconut

Break up biscuits − not powdery but not too big.

Melt butter. Add icing sugar, cocoa and coconut and mix well.

Blend in beaten eggs; fold in broken biscuits.

Press mixture into foil-lined tray (about 30cm x 25cm). Refrigerate to set before icing.

For the icing, sift sugar and cocoa into bowl. Add butter and water and mix until smooth.

Spread on slice and sprinkle with coconut.

When set, cut into squares.

Reader Kerry Herbison

"Good chocolate isn't an indulgence; it isn't wicked, or naughty, or sinful. It's simply a necessity, because it has the power to make you feel better, not bitter, about life. Turn it into rich, gooey, delectably dark brownies in which the energy-giving sweetness is controlled by the innate bitterness, and give yourself up to its healing power."

White chocolate and cranberry cookies

Buttery, oaty, chewy biscuits with nuggets of white chocolate and tart-but-sweet cranberries.

200g butter, softened
1 cup packed brown sugar
½ cup condensed milk
1 egg
1½ tsp vanilla essence
1½ cups plain flour
1 tsp baking soda
2 cups rolled oats
1¼ cups dried cranberries (or raisins)
1 cup white chocolate bits

Preheat oven to 180C.

Cream butter, sugar and condensed milk. Add egg and vanilla and beat until mixture is light and fluffy.

Sift flour and baking soda into creamed mixture. Stir in rolled oats, cranberries and white chocolate bits. Place tablespoons on greased oven trays and press down with a fork.

Bake for about 15 minutes, until golden.
Makes 35-40

Reader Jo Utting

Chewy chocolate chunk slice

Recipes made with condensed milk are often rich, sweet and more-ish. This is no exception. A bit like a brownie, a bit like a slice, these choc-chunk studded squares are easy to make and very, very easy to eat. We couldn't stop at just one!

1 cup self-raising flour
½ cup desiccated coconut
½ cup brown sugar
2 tbsp cocoa powder
125g butter, melted
1 x 395g tin condensed milk
100g dark chocolate
100g white chocolate
½ cup chopped nuts such as walnuts, pecans or macadamia nuts (optional)
icing sugar, to dust (optional)

Preheat oven to 180C. Grease and line the sides of a 22cm square tin or equivalent (e.g. a lamington tin.)
   Combine flour, coconut, sugar, cocoa powder, butter and condensed milk in a large bowl and mix well. Spread mixture into the prepared pan.
   Roughly chop the dark and white chocolate into chunks and press into base. Sprinkle nuts over base (if using).
   Bake for about 25 minutes. Make sure it's still a little soft when taking out of oven (the softer it is, the more fudgy it is!).
   Remove from oven and cool in the pan. Cut into squares. Dust with icing sugar to serve, if desired.
Makes 16 pieces

Reader Linda Nguyen

Mocha hazelnut crescents

A lighter, nuttier cousin of traditional shortbread, these biscuits are nice with or without the chocolate coating.

150g butter
¼ cup castor sugar
1 cup plain flour
½ cup self-raising flour
½ cup hazelnut meal
2 tsp granulated instant coffee (yes, instant coffee,
    and must be granulated to give crunch)
150g dark cooking chocolate
¼ cup extra hazelnut meal

Preheat oven to 180C. Line a biscuit tray with baking paper.
    Cream butter and sugar. Sift in flours, meal and coffee powder. Knead to form a soft dough.
    Shape the dough into crescents (two teaspoons of dough per biscuit).
    Bake 15-20 minutes. Cool on rack, then dip half of each biscuit into melted chocolate and coat with meal. Place in fridge to set chocolate.
Makes 24

Note: These biscuits keep well in the freezer.

Reader Allison Clarke

"Sludge" slice

This simple slice combines a coconut-rough style topping with an unexpected minty flavour. And the name? "This family favourite was once just known as 'chocolate slice', until one day one of the children said 'that reminds me of sludge up near the dam'. The name stuck," explains Erna Howell. "I always tripled the recipe — it freezes well and also keeps for weeks in a cool cupboard or fridge."

125g butter
½ cup sugar
1 tbsp golden syrup
1 cup desiccated coconut
1 cup self-raising flour

Topping

60g butter
⅓ tin (about 130g) condensed milk
1 cup icing sugar
1 tbsp cocoa
¾ cup desiccated coconut
½ tsp peppermint essence (or to taste)

Preheat oven to 180C.

Cream butter and sugar, add syrup, then coconut, then flour. Press into a greased 18cm x 28cm tin. Bake for about 20 minutes. Do not overcook.

While base is cooking, prepare the topping. Melt butter and condensed milk together, then mix in icing sugar, cocoa, coconut and peppermint essence. Pour topping over base while the base is still hot and the topping still warm. Allow to cool before cutting into slices. Makes about 24-30 pieces

Erna Howell, Reader

Marshmallow slice

One for marshmallow lovers – a soft, cakey, not-too-sweet base topped with a layer of soft marshmallow and a scattering of cherries and nuts.

200g self-raising flour
2 slightly rounded tbsp cocoa powder
125g soft margarine
½ cup castor sugar
1 large egg, separated
2-3 tsp water (if needed)
½ cup icing sugar
8-10 glacé cherries (each into about 6 pieces)
2 tbsp crushed peanuts

Preheat oven to 175C.

For the base, sift flour and cocoa, then rub in margarine.

Mix in castor sugar and egg yolk.

If mixture doesn't hold together when pressed, add a little water, a teaspoonful at a time.

Tip into a lined or greased slice tray, spread evenly then press down.

For the topping, beat egg white until soft peaks form. Stir in icing sugar in three or four lots, beating with each addition. Spread over base.

Sprinkle evenly with chopped cherries and nuts.

Bake for approximately 20 minutes; check midway through – if the meringue is browning, cover with foil.

Cool and cut into squares when ready to serve.

Reader Zola Maylor

Chocolate orange butter biscuits

Beverley Sutherland Smith's cooking column appeared in the very first stand-alone edition of Epicure in March 1986. These small, crisp, buttery biscuits were among the hundreds of recipes she shared with Epicure readers over the next 10 years.

125g butter
125g sugar
grated rind of 1 orange
1 tbsp cocoa
1 egg yolk
125g plain flour
pinch salt

Preheat oven to 170C.

Chop the butter into chunky pieces and put in a bowl with the sugar. Cream until fluffy (it's important to cream the butter and sugar well or the biscuits can taste sugary).

Add orange rind and mix through. Sift the cocoa over the top and stir into the creamed mixture. Add the egg yolk. Sift the flour and salt over the top and mix well. It will be quite a soft mixture, but not so sticky that you cannot handle it.

Take teaspoons of the mixture and roll into balls between your hands. Flatten down with a fork. If sticky, dip the fork into a little flour but shake away any excess.

Place on a baking tray and bake for about 15 minutes until firm. They will crisp more as they cool. Leave on the tray for a couple of minutes, then transfer to a cake rack and leave until completely cold. Store in an airtight tin.

Makes 30

Columnist Beverley Sutherland Smith, 1987

Almond honey slice

Almond honey slice

250g butter
⅔ cup castor sugar
⅓ cup honey
⅓ cup cream
⅓ cup brandy
300g flaked almonds
150g unsalted shelled pistachio nuts
100g dark or milk chocolate

Preheat oven to 200C. Line the base and sides of a 19cm x 29cm lamington tin with baking paper and grease well.

In a large saucepan, melt the butter, add the sugar, honey, cream and brandy. Stir and bring to the boil. Remove from heat and add the nuts. Mix well.

Spread the mixture into the prepared tin and bake for 25 minutes or until the top is golden brown. (Place a dish in the bottom of the oven to catch any overflowing liquid during cooking.) Remove and cool.

Melt the chocolate in a bowl over gently simmering water. Drizzle over the slice. Refrigerate. Cut into squares or rectangles to serve and store in the fridge.
Makes about 16 pieces

Columnist Luke Mangan, 2002

Geoff's apricot slice

It sounds as if it will be too, too sweet – but it isn't. And it doesn't need baking, either, so this crunchy, coconutty treat is very easy to make.

250g packet plain sweet biscuits
15g butter
1 x 395g tin condensed milk
375g packet dried apricots, roughly chopped
1 cup desiccated coconut
2 x 240g blocks white chocolate

Line a 20cm square baking tray with baking paper.

Roughly crush biscuits. Melt butter and condensed milk in a small saucepan over low heat. Mix biscuits, apricots and coconut in a large bowl. Add melted butter and milk and stir to combine well.

Pat out mix in baking tray and refrigerate to set.

Ice thickly with melted white chocolate. Slice into squares when set.

Reader Louise Staley

Kamikaze brownies

300g bittersweet chocolate (or couverture)
125g unsalted butter
3 large eggs
1 cup brown sugar
1 tbsp liqueur or brandy (e.g. Grand Marnier or Tia Maria)
½ cup plain flour OR very finely ground nuts (walnuts, hazelnuts, almonds, cashews, etc)

Preheat oven to 180C. Grease and line a 23cm square cake tin.

Melt the chocolate and butter together over simmering water until smooth. Let cool slightly. Beat the eggs with the sugar until thick and light. Add the liqueur. Gently fold in the chocolate-butter mixture. Fold in the flour or ground nuts. Pour batter into tin. Bake for about 20-25 minutes. It is best to underbake these so keep an eye on them after about 15 minutes. They should test done around the edges but still be soft in the centre. You can let them cook a little longer if you prefer them to be cakey (I prefer them to be fudgy). The brownies will not rise much at all as there is no baking powder in the batter, so don't be alarmed.

Let cool in tin for about 10 minutes then carefully invert onto a wire rack and cool. When cool, cut into squares.

Variations
1. If using Grand Marnier, add the finely grated zest of an orange as well.
2. Use strong black coffee instead of liqueur or substitute a teaspoon of vanilla essence instead.
3. You can also add a cup of roughly chopped chocolate to the batter or sprinkled over the top before baking. If you do, let them cool completely in the pan and leave them for at least a few hours so the chocolate has time to set again.

Reader Viviane Buzzi

Brownies from the cupboard

Here, Celia Brissenden shares a recipe inspired by one published some time ago in Epicure. "They can be made with in-the-cupboard ingredients (i.e. cocoa, not chocolate) and they are even gooier and denser than the original." This cocoa-based brownie has a nicely crusty top and moist middle, and provides edible evidence that a cocoa-based brownie can be just as rich and indulgent as one made with chocolate.

1 cup unsalted butter
1 cup sifted cocoa
1 cup raw sugar
1 cup castor sugar
4 large eggs
½ cup plain flour
½ cup almond meal (whiz almonds in a blender to make instant, fresh meal. There's no need to skin them)
1 cup chopped nuts of choice
1 tsp vanilla essence
¼ tsp salt

Preheat oven to 180C. Butter and flour a 20cm square tin and line bottom with baking paper.

Melt butter in large bowl (or melt then transfer to large bowl). Stir in cocoa, then sugars. Mix in eggs one at a time. Add flour and almond meal and stir in well. Add nuts, vanilla and salt.

Place mixture in tin and smooth down. Bake for 20 minutes, then test with a skewer – there should be a few moist crumbs. It may need up to another 10 minutes.

Leave to cool and shrink in the tin slightly before turning out onto a cooling rack.

Reader Celia Brissenden

Choc-top caramel slice

Mary Faulkner's version of a recipe she once saw on the side of a tin of condensed milk produces a rich, buttery base, a rich caramel middle and a rich, smooth chocolate top – in other words, a very rich, delicious and indulgent treat. "The slices will last for several weeks if kept in an air-tight container in the refrigerator – if the kids don't find them!" says Mary.

Base
125g unsalted butter
1 cup plain flour
½ cup brown sugar, lightly packed
½ cup desiccated coconut
Caramel
25g butter (about 2 tbsp)
2 tbsp golden syrup
1 x 400g can of Nestle condensed milk
Chocolate topping
125g dark chocolate, such as Club or Old Gold, chopped
60g copha

Preheat oven to 180C. Lightly grease a 28 x 18cm tin.

To make the base, melt butter, add flour, sugar and coconut, and mix well. Press mixture into tin and bake for 25-30 minutes.

While the base is cooking, make the caramel. Melt the butter, take off heat and stir in the golden syrup and condensed milk. Mix well then pour over the cooked base and return to the oven to for another 20 minutes. Take out of oven and set aside to cool.

To make the topping, melt chocolate and copha in a bowl over a pan of simmering water, or use the microwave on medium for about 2 minutes. Mix well and pour over the cooled base, then chill in the refrigerator. When cold, cut into small slices using a hot knife.

Reader Mary Faulkner

Valmai Hall's chocolate coconut fingers

"One of the unwritten rules of our biannual family holidays in Port Elliott, South Australia in the '60s and '70s was that Mum would always make three batches of biscuits to take with us – monte carlos, almond butter biscuits and a chocolate slice. These were inevitably demolished within a week. Well, we had our reasons: three kids, all that running around in the sea air and swimming and, most significantly, my father's serious sweet tooth. I had a minor preference for the chocolate slice, the start of a lifetime chocolate love affair. My sister Julianne favoured the butter biscuits; my older brother Chris was completely undiscerning, devouring anything in sight. So like a boy."

1 cup cornflakes
1 cup desiccated coconut, plus extra for sprinkling
1 cup self-raising flour
½ tsp vanilla essence
½ cup brown sugar
1 tbsp cocoa
150g margarine, melted
Chocolate icing
4 heaped tbsp icing sugar
1 heaped tbsp cocoa
1 tsp cinnamon
1 dsstsp butter, melted

Preheat oven to 180C.

Mix all dry ingredients plus vanilla and pour margarine over. Mix and press into a flat, greased rectangular lamington tin. Bake for 10-15 minutes.

While hot, ice with chocolate icing and sprinkle with desiccated coconut. (To make the icing, sift the icing sugar, cocoa and cinnamon and mix with butter and a small quantity of hot water. Add more icing sugar if too thin.)

Slice into fingers when cool.

Epicure deputy editor Necia Wilden

Chocolate drops

These chewy, nutty and easy-to-make macaroons represent the wonderful tradition of fundraising recipe books. Christine Cramer contributed this recipe to the Nhill Hospital Ladies' Auxiliary Recipe Book, which was first printed in the 1950s and proved so popular it was reprinted several times. Now 94 and still living in Nhill, she generously agreed to allow the recipe to be reprinted here, after it was recommended by an Epicure reader.

2 egg whites
pinch salt
6 rounded tbsp castor sugar
1 rounded tbsp cornflour
1 rounded tbsp cocoa
½ tsp vanilla
½ cup chopped nuts
½ cup desiccated coconut

Preheat oven to 180C.

Beat egg whites and salt until stiff; add sugar gradually and beat until sugar is dissolved and meringue holds its shape. Beat in cornflour and cocoa.

Remove beater, fold in vanilla, nuts and coconut. Drop heaped teaspoonfuls onto greased tray and decorate with nuts. Bake for 30-35 minutes.
Makes 25-30

Christine Cramer

Munchies

"When my great aunt, Doris Little, moved house some years ago, I inherited a pile of old recipes. This is a variation of one which came written on a scrap of yellowing paper."

115g butter
¾ cup of packed brown sugar
1 egg, lightly beaten
grated rind of one orange
1 tbsp orange juice
⅓ cup of roughly chopped hazelnuts
⅓ cup dark choc bits
¾ cup self-raising flour
½ tsp bicarb soda
1 cup rolled oats

Preheat oven to 180C. Position racks in the top half of the oven.

Cream butter and sugar with an electric beater. Remove beater. Add beaten egg, orange rind and juice, nuts and chocolate and mix well with a wooden spoon. Sift flour and bicarb soda into bowl and mix in. Fold in the oats.

Drop spoonfuls onto baking paper-lined trays (the biscuits spread during cooking, so space them out). Cook for 9-10 minutes, rotating the trays after 5 minutes to ensure even cooking. (If you are baking two trays at once, the biscuits will take about 10 minutes; if you bake one tray at a time — and I find the biscuits turn out better this way — the cooking time is a little less).
Makes about 22

Kylie Walker, Epicure Editor

Chocolate espresso brownies

Serve as a dessert with ice-cream or cream, or cut into smaller squares to have with coffee. Also nice drizzled with chocolate sauce.

200g bitter dark chocolate, chopped
200g butter
4 eggs
200g castor sugar
2 tbsp espresso or very strong black coffee
200g plain flour, sifted
¼ tsp salt

Preheat oven to 180C. Line a small baking pan or roasting tray (about 25cm x 20cm) with buttered foil or greaseproof paper.

Melt the chocolate and butter, stirring until smooth. Remove from the heat and allow to cool for 10 minutes.

In a large bowl, beat the eggs and sugar with a hand-held electric mixer until pale. Beat in the coffee and then the half-cooled chocolate mixture. Fold in the sifted flour and salt.

Pour the batter into the pan and bake for 20-25 minutes. It should be crusty on top but still a bit gooey inside. Leave to cool in the pan. Serve just-warm, or cold, cut into squares.
Makes 12

Jill Dupleix, 2004

Nat's best-ever brownies

Natalie Paull, of baking business Little Bertha, spent years perfecting her favourite brownie recipe, which she says can be eaten as is or heated and served as a pudding with vanilla ice-cream "and chocolate sauce, to be extra indulgent". Beating in all the cream cheese makes a rich, gooey brownie; gently folding in larger pieces of cream cheese gives a pretty, but still moist, brownie.

4 large eggs
360g castor sugar
180g raw walnuts or pecans
320g salted butter
130g dark chocolate
120g plain flour
80g Dutch cocoa
160g cream cheese, chilled
optional flavours – 2 tbsp strong espresso or
    grated zest of one orange

Preheat oven to 160C. Line an 18cm x 28cm lamington tin with baking paper.

Using the mixer bowl and paddle, beat the eggs, sugar and nuts for 2 minutes on low speed.

While it is mixing, melt the butter and pour over the chocolate and stir to melt it. Add the coffee or orange to the choc-butter mix at this point, if using.

Scrape the choc mix into the egg mix and combine on low speed for 2 minutes.

Sift together the flour and cocoa. Add flour mix to the mixer bowl and mix for 2 minutes. At this point the batter should begin to look matte and creamy – if it is still dark and glossy, mix it for longer. Break off marble-sized pieces of the cream cheese and place into mix. Beat for 20-30 seconds (or gently mix in with a spatula).

Scrape mixture into tin. Bake about 30 minutes or until fine cracks begin to appear on the surface and the edges are starting to puff a little.

Pastry cook Natalie Paull, 2005

My ultimate choc-chip cookies

Matt Preston's writing always draws a big response from readers. When he published the first version of this rich, buttery, chunky cookie, some readers loved it – but others didn't. "Perfect," said one reader. "Too buttery," said another. So Matt went back to the kitchen, and a few weeks later Epicure published this even chunkier version.

600g chocolate of your choice (dark, white, milk or any combination)
2 cups plain flour (75 per cent wholemeal gives an appealingly earthy –
    but not overly so – texture; this is a democratic biscuit, so you decide)
1 tsp salt
1 tsp baking powder
250g well-softened unsalted butter
$\frac{2}{3}$ cup light brown sugar
$\frac{1}{4}$ cup dark brown sugar
$\frac{2}{3}$ cup granulated white sugar
1 tsp vanilla essence
2 tbsp water
1 egg
125g almonds, roughly chopped
125g macadamia nuts, roughly chopped
125g skinless hazelnuts, roughly chopped (if you prefer to leave the nuts
    out, replace with more chocolate)

Preheat oven to 180C.
    Break the chocolate into squares, about 2cm each. You want the milk or dark chocolate hunks to be bigger than the white ones because they'll melt more when cooked and if too small they'll disappear. Set aside.
    Sift together the flour, salt and baking powder into a bowl.
    Using a mixer, cream the butter and mix in the three types of sugar. Add the vanilla essence, water and egg. Beat together.
    Beat in the flour mixture. Stir in the chocolate hunks and the nuts. The mixture should come away from the sides of the bowl to form a ball. If it is still too sticky, add a little flour.
    Drop balls of the mixture, well spaced, onto a baking tray lined with nonstick baking parchment. Use a dessertspoon for big bikkies or a teaspoon for smaller ones. Cook for about 10 minutes or until almost golden.
    Eat some immediately.
    Let the rest, um, er, rest and then cool on a wire rack.

Writer Matt Preston, 2003

Maw's chocolate apricot slice

This light, cake-like slice studded with ginger and fruit was a recipe inherited by Susie Rogers from her mother, Margaret, known to the family as "Maw".

90g dried apricots, chopped
1½ cups self-raising flour
1½ tbsp cocoa
¼ tsp cinnamon
pinch salt
120g butter
¾ cup sugar
60g chopped nuts (usually walnuts)
2 tbsp crystallised ginger, chopped
90g dried apricots, chopped
2 eggs, beaten
½ cup milk
chopped peanuts (or other nuts), to decorate

Preheat oven to 180C.
    Soak apricots in boiling water for half an hour.
    Mix flour, cocoa, cinnamon and salt.
    Melt butter and pour on. Add sugar, nuts, ginger and drained apricots. Fold in egg and milk.
    Spread in swiss roll tin (20cm x 30cm) and bake for 30 minutes.
    Ice with chocolate icing (see page 178) and decorate with nuts.

Reader Susie Rogers

cakes057

Chocolate sponge

"This recipe was given to me by my mother 46 years ago," says Joan Bateman. "It never fails!" The toasted coconut on top adds a nice touch to this light sponge.

3 eggs, separated
½ cup sugar
1 tbsp golden syrup
½ cup cornflour
½ tsp bicarb soda
½ tsp cream of tartar
1 tsp plain flour
1 heaped dsstsp cocoa
whipped cream, for assembly
½ cup desiccated coconut

Preheat oven to 180C. Grease two 20cm sponge tins.

Beat the egg whites until stiff. Add the yolks one at a time, beating well after each addition. Gradually add the sugar and continue beating until dissolved. Beat in the golden syrup.

Sift the dry ingredients three times and then fold into the mixture. Divide the mixture between the two sponge tins. Bake for 20 minutes. Remove from oven and cool in tins.

When cool, remove from tins and sandwich together with whipped cream. Ice with chocolate icing (see page 178) and sprinkle toasted coconut over the top.

Reader Joan Bateman

White chocolate and cherry Cointreau cake

A moist cake studded with chewy fruit that can be enjoyed by the slice or served as a lovely dessert with thick cream or cherries – or both.

⅓ cup sour dried cherries
¼ cup Cointreau
3 eggs, separated
⅔ cup castor sugar
200g white chocolate
125g butter, unsalted
¾ cup plain flour, sifted

Soak cherries in Cointreau for 1 hour.
   Preheat oven to 170C. Line a 20cm shallow cake tin with baking paper.
   Beat egg yolks with castor sugar until pale in colour.
   Melt the chocolate in a bowl over hot water, making sure the bowl does not touch the water.
   Whisk the butter into the melted chocolate. Then fold the chocolate into the yolk mixture.
   Using a wide spatula, fold the cherries and Cointreau into the mix, followed by the flour.
   Beat the egg whites to stiff peaks and fold gently through.
   Pour into the cake tin and bake for 45-55 minutes or until a skewer comes out clean. If the cake is browning too much during cooking, cover the top with baking paper or foil.
   The cake should be slightly soft to the touch and moist in texture.
   Cool before turning out.
   Serve with thick double cream.

Reader Emma Pears

A well-travelled wedding cake

Nancy Telfer has made this lovely moist mud cake for many occasions, but the recent wedding of a friend required a little more effort than most – the cakes were made in Melbourne, taken to Tasmania carefully packed in hand-luggage and iced on the wedding morn. Flowers from the bride's garden, picked by children among the guests, provided decorations. "It was a great wedding – and everyone seemed to leave with a smudge of chocolate icing on them somewhere," says Nancy.

1 ½ cups strong brewed coffee
¼ cup brandy
150g dark chocolate
250g unsalted butter
2 cups castor sugar
2 cups plain flour
1 tsp bicarb soda
small pinch salt
2 eggs, beaten
1 tsp vanilla essence

Preheat oven to 135C.

Place coffee, brandy, chocolate and butter in a medium saucepan over a low heat and stir until smooth. Remove from heat and add castor sugar. Stir to combine. Allow the mixture to cool slightly (about 10 minutes).

Place the mixture in an electric mixer bowl. Sift flour with bicarb soda and salt. Add to mixture slowly, mixing well between additions.

Add the eggs and vanilla and beat until smooth.

Place mixture in a 20cm tin and bake until a skewer inserted in the centre comes out clean, about 1½ hours.

Allow to cool in tin on a wire rack.

Decorate with chocolate ganache (see page 178), or make an icing by melting 125g unsalted butter with 125g dark chocolate. Cool, then beat until thick and spreadable.

Reader Nancy Telfer

Hero cake

"This cake has been baked in my husband's family since World War I," says Elizabeth Brookes. "His late grandmother, Muriel Stennett, made it for soldiers during the war. Muriel's daughter, the late Peggy Brookes, continued to make it for all special family occasions, from the 1950s until the 1990s. Now I make it for birthdays – and even my son has made it." This is a light, spicy cake with a hint of chocolate from the cocoa.

1 heaped cup self-raising flour
½ tsp cinnamon
½ tsp ginger
¾ dsstsp allspice
1 tbsp cocoa
2 tbsp butter
1 cup of sugar
4 eggs, beaten
2 tbsp milk
Filling
1 cup icing sugar
¾ tsp vanilla essence
melted butter

Preheat oven to 180C. Grease two 17cm round tins.

Sift flour with spices and cocoa. Cream butter and sugar. Mix in eggs. Add sifted dry ingredients and milk and mix. Put mixture in tin and cook for 15-20 minutes.

When cool, join with buttery filling made by mixing icing sugar, vanilla and melted butter (enough to make paste).

Dust icing sugar on top.

Reader Elizabeth Brookes

Max's flourless peach cake

"This is an intense, moist and easy to make cake, and forms a lovely caramelised crust on the outside," says Max Sargent of his recipe. Like many good recipes, this one had several sources of inspiration – the original idea, he says, came from an orange cake recipe in Claudia Roden's classic cookbook, *A Book of Middle Eastern Food*, and the soured milk component from a recipe that appeared in Epicure's "My Favourite Chocolate Cake" series some years ago.

225g ground almonds
225g granulated or brown sugar
6 tbsp cocoa
1 tsp bicarb soda
½ cup milk soured with juice of one lemon
2 eggs
one handful of chopped dried peach

Preheat oven to 175C. Grease and line a 20cm round tin.
   Mix dry ingredients, add wet ones and mix well to combine.
Pour batter into tin and bake for 45 minutes.
   If desired, serve with grilled peach slices.

Variation: Replace dried peaches with two handfuls of pitted fresh cherries. Allow an extra 10 minutes of cooking time.

Reader Max Sargent

Manzi's flourless hazelnut cake

A moist, dense cake with a lovely hazelnut flavor. "This recipe was given to me by Manzi Valent, my late mother-in-law, who was Jewish-Hungarian. She then lived in Czechoslovakia, and came to Australia in 1949. She was an excellent cook!" says Julie Valent. "The original recipe was without flour, and thus for observant Jews can be eaten during passover."

150g hazelnuts
200g good quality dark eating chocolate
100g butter
200g sugar
5 eggs
100g self-raising flour (optional)

Preheat oven to 180C.
    Roast hazelnuts in oven, rub off skins, leave to cool completely, then grind coarsely.
    Melt chocolate on a plate over hot water. Cool slightly.
    Cream together butter and sugar in a mixing bowl. Beat in the eggs, one by one. If using flour, add between the eggs. Stir in melted chocolate. Lastly, add hazelnuts.
    Place mixture in a 25cm round tin and bake until just firm, about 30-40 minutes.
    Cool in tin. Dust with icing sugar to serve.

Variation: The addition of flour simply makes the cake a little firmer. It can easily be omitted for a flourless version.

Reader Julie Valent

Dutch chocolate cake

"This is quite unusual but absolutely delicious," says Meredith Rogers, of a recipe her mother originally found in a Cadbury's Bournville Cocoa® advertisement many years ago. The cake is moist and solid (but not gluggy) with firm slices of apple.

125g softened butter
½ cup castor sugar
1 egg, lightly beaten
1 cup self-raising flour
2 tbsp cocoa
¼ cup milk
2 tbsp sultanas
2 apples, peeled, cored, halved and finely sliced
melted butter
ground cinnamon

Preheat oven to 180C. Grease and line a 20cm cake tin.
    Place butter, sugar, egg, flour, cocoa and milk into the bowl of a mixer and beat slowly until combined. Increase speed and beat for 2 minutes.
    Spread half the mixture into tin (Meredith notes that the batter can be stiff and sometimes needs "persuading"). Cover with sultanas and most of the sliced apple, reserving a few slices to decorate the top. Top with remaining cake mixture. Decorate with reserved apple slices. Brush with melted butter and sprinkle with cinnamon. Bake for 45-50 minutes until a skewer inserted in the centre comes clean. Allow to cool in tin for 10 minutes before turning out onto wire rack to cool.
    Delicious served just warm with whipped cream.

Variation: In a 20cm tin, this makes quite a low cake. We suggest a slightly smaller tin size, which would also make it easier to spread the thick batter. Just allow a little extra cooking time.

Reader Meredith Rogers
This recipe appears with the permission of Cadbury Schweppes.

Kentish nut cake

Is this a cake, or a slice, we wondered. We're still not sure. The result has a fine crumb with a hint of cocoa, and a slightly crisp crust.

150g SR flour
pinch of salt
1 desspn cocoa
120g butter
120g castor sugar
2 eggs
1 tbsp chopped walnuts
2 tbsp desiccated coconut
4½ tbsp milk
icing sugar, to decorate

Preheat oven to 180C.
　　Sift flour, salt and cocoa.
　　Cream butter and sugar. Beat in eggs, one at a time.
　　Add walnuts and coconut.
　　Fold in sifted ingredients, alternatively with milk.
　　Bake in a 20cm square cake tin in 180C oven for 40 minutes.
　　When cooled, dust with icing sugar to serve.

Variation: To notch up the chocolate factor, this can be covered with a simple chocolate icing.

Reader Janet Young

Proodie's big chocolate cake

A great example of the way recipes pass along chains of friendship, this recipe was given to Angela Perry by her friend Prue Catchlove, who got it from her friend Anne Walkom. "I have modified the recipe in the intervening years," Angela says. "It is the best cake for a big crowd – no icing required and always a hit." Moist and light, it is also easy to make and, as it can be abandoned for hours in the middle, good for cooks juggling busy schedules.

250g butter
6 tbsp cocoa
3 cups sugar
1½ cups water
1 tsp bicarb soda
4 eggs
3 cups self-raising flour

Place butter, cocoa, sugar and water in a medium-sized saucepan and cook over low heat until sugar has dissolved. Bring to boil and simmer for 5 minutes. Remove from heat and cool for 5-10 minutes. Add bicarb soda and stir briskly (to prevent the mixture fizzing up). Allow to cool for half an hour (you can leave alone for several hours at this point if that suits you).
　　While mixture is cooling, preheat oven to 175C.
　　Line a large deep baking tray or lasagne dish (approximately 20cm x 32cm) with baking paper. Spray with oil.
　　Pour mixture into large bowl. Quickly beat in the eggs, one at a time. Add flour and whisk in quickly. Do not overbeat. Put into dish.
　　Bake for about 50 minutes, or until a skewer inserted in the centre comes out clean. Cool for 10 minutes in pan before turning out onto a rack. When cool, invert and dust with icing sugar to serve.

Reader Angela Perry

Coco the burlesque wonder cake

"This cake gets fan mail," says Ben Johnson, one of Epicure's more far-flung readers. Born in Melbourne and now based in Los Angeles, he runs a website called thelovebite.com. Half date advisor and half cookbook, the site shares recipes with intriguing names such as Adam's Ruin, Mr Lash and of course, this tempting number, which features a wicked choc-studded frosting.

175g unsalted butter, softened
⅓ cup cocoa
⅔ cup castor sugar
1½ cups self-raising flour
1 tsp baking powder
½ cup golden syrup
¾ cup light sour cream
2 eggs

Frosting
50g butter, softened
½ cup sour cream
3 tbsp golden syrup
80g melted dark chocolate
3 cups icing sugar
¼ cup cocoa
25g additional dark chocolate, broken into pieces

Preheat oven to 200C. Butter and flour a 20-23cm round cake tin.

Blend butter, cocoa, sugar, flour, baking powder, golden syrup, sour cream and eggs in a food processor until well blended. Pour batter into the tin.

Bake for 10 minutes; reduce heat to 180C and bake for another 30 minutes. If cake bounces back when tapped lightly on top, it's done (the exact cooking time will vary depending on the size of the cake tin).

Let cool in the pan for 5-10 minutes before turning out.

To make frosting: blend butter, sour cream, golden syrup, melted chocolate, icing sugar and cocoa in food processor until whipped. Add the extra chocolate pieces and pulse the processor to splinter them into choc chips in the frosting. Spread over cooled cake.

Reader Ben Johnson

Double chocolate
muffins

Double chocolate muffins

1¾ cups self-raising flour
¾ cup castor sugar
¼ cup cocoa (good quality Dutch cocoa works best)
1½ cups dark chocolate melts, broken up
2 eggs, lightly beaten
½ cup sunflower oil
¾ cup milk

Preheat oven to 180C.

Sift flour, sugar and cocoa into a large bowl. Add chocolate melts, egg, oil and milk. Mix until all ingredients are just combined. Do not over mix.

Place muffin-size paper liners into a muffin tray. Spoon mixture into cups so each is about three-quarters full. Bake for 18-20 minutes.
Makes 12-15 muffins

Reader Caren Vidler

Melt, mix, bung chocolate cake

A never-fail, whatever-the-occasion chocolate-cake-in-a-flash. Make it as cupcakes or as one big cake.

3 tbsp butter
1 cup self-raising flour
2 tbsp cocoa
1 cup castor sugar
2 eggs
½ cup milk
1 tsp vanilla essence

Preheat oven to 180C.

Melt butter, mix with remaining ingredients until smooth, bung in the oven in a lined or well-greased 20cm cake tin for about 20 minutes or individual patty pans for around 5-10 minutes. Cool.

Top with a simple chocolate icing or − easier still on a freshly baked cake − dust with icing sugar.

Columnist Miranda Sharp, 2002

"There's something very satisfying about baking. It's not just eating the results – it's the aroma in the house, it's the hospitality. People get a sense of pride in bringing out something they've baked. It's a loving, caring gesture ... People who may not cook much will still bake a cake for someone."

Beverley Sutherland Smith

The Woolnough family chocolate cake

A deliciously moist cake. A simple whipped cream also works
well as a filling.

250ml water
330g sugar
125g butter
20g cocoa
1 tsp bicarb soda
225g self-raising flour, sifted
2 eggs, lightly beaten

Mock cream
80g softened butter
80g castor sugar
3 tbsp milk (luke warm)
1 tbsp boiling water
Chocolate coating
120ml cream
100g dark chocolate

Preheat oven to 160C. Lightly grease a 20cm square cake pan and line with baking paper.

Place water and sugar in saucepan. Heat and stir until sugar dissolves, add butter and cocoa, bring to boil and simmer for 1 minute. Remove from heat and add bicarb soda. Allow to cool for 5 minutes, then add sifted flour and eggs and mix well. Pour into prepared pan and bake for 40 minutes.

Allow to cool and then split cake through centre.

For the mock cream, cream butter and sugar very thoroughly (until white). While still beating, add milk very slowly. When smooth, very slowly add boiling water.

Bring cream to boil, add chocolate and stir until smooth. Cool slightly.

To assemble, fill cake with cream, then cover with chocolate coating.

The finished cake can be stored in the freezer. Defrost at room temperature.

Reader Edna Woolnough

Chocolate chip cake

"I've been making this for years, much to my children's enjoyment," wrote Caren when she sent us this recipe. In America, you'll find many variations on this enticingly named cake. A lot are based on packet mixes, other made from scratch. Some use brown sugar, some castor sugar. Some are iced, some aren't. Some throw all the chocolate chips into the batter, others layer them as Caren does in this recipe.

125g softened butter
1 cup castor sugar
2 eggs
300g sour cream
1½ cups plain flour
1½ tsp baking powder
1 tsp bicarb soda
250g dark chocolate melts, broken in half
1 tbsp white sugar

Preheat oven to 180C. Grease and line a 6cm deep, 20cm square cake tin.

Using an electric mixer, beat butter and castor sugar until creamy. Beat in eggs one at a time. Stir in sour cream. Sift flour, baking powder and bicarb soda over butter mixture. Fold in until just combined. Spread two thirds of batter over base of prepared tin. Sprinkle with half the chocolate melts. Top with remaining batter then the rest of the chocolate. Sprinkle with white sugar.

Bake for 45-50 minutes or until a skewer inserted in the centre comes out clean.

Allow to cool slightly in tin before removing to rack.

To serve, dust with icing sugar.

Reader Caren Vilder

Chocolate honey cake

A delightful honey aroma fills the kitchen as this bakes. The result – Diana Wolf's adaptation of a recipe by writer Rita Erlich – is a moist, flavoursome cake that showcases the flavour of the honey used.

2 eggs
1 cup vegetable oil (or canola)
¾ cup honey
1 cup sugar
1 tbsp marmalade (or grated rind of one orange)
1 tsp vanilla essence
pinch salt
2 tbsp cocoa powder, mixed with 2-3 tbsp boiling water
   and cooled
1 cup self-raising flour
1 cup plain flour
1 tsp ground cinnamon
½ tsp mixed spice
1 tsp ground ginger
1 tsp instant coffee powder
½ tsp bicarb soda
1 cup boiling water

Preheat oven to 180 degrees. Grease a 23cm cake tin and line with baking paper.

Mix together eggs, oil, honey, sugar, marmalade, vanilla and cocoa paste.

Sift or mix together flours, spices, salt and coffee powder. Add to wet mixture, stir well. It will be very thick. Lastly, dissolve bicarb soda in boiling water. Add carefully and mix well. Pour into tin (don't worry if it looks runny). Bake in the centre of the oven for about 70 minutes, or until a toothpick inserted in the centre comes out clean.

Allow to cool completely before storing.

Variation: Nuts, sultanas or raisins (about three tablespoons) can be added. Sprinkle with a little flour and add after the boiling water has been mixed in.

Reader Diana Wolf

Flourless chocolate cupcakes

A cupcake for grown-ups with a not-too-sweet flavour and a piece of rich couverture chocolate hidden in the centre.

125g unsalted butter, softened

½ cup dark brown sugar

1 tsp pure vanilla bean paste (or essence)

3 eggs

½ cup unsweetened cocoa (e.g. Green & Blacks)

1½ tsp baking powder

125g almond meal

1 tbsp vanilla yoghurt

2 tbsp amaretto liqueur

12 pieces of dark couverture (or good quality dark chocolate, at least 70 per cent cocoa)

Ganache

100g dark couverture or good quality bittersweet chocolate

1 tbsp liqueur, strong coffee or 2 tsp pure vanilla essence

150ml double cream (at least 48 per cent butterfat)

Preheat oven to 180C. Line 12 muffin pans with cupcake/muffin paper cups. Do not grease.

Beat together the butter, sugar and vanilla until smooth and light. Beat in eggs, one at a time, until batter is smooth.

Sift in cocoa and baking powder and beat.

Fold in two-thirds of the almond meal until well mixed. Add the yoghurt and amaretto and beat well. Fold in the remaining almond meal.

Fill the cupcake pans to full with the batter. In each, place a piece of the chocolate and press down a little so that it sits in the middle of the batter. Bake for 25 minutes, until cooked but not dry.

These are wonderful served warm with coffee. To make them special, swirl on some chocolate ganache and decorate as desired.

To make ganache: chop the chocolate finely or grate into a heatproof bowl. Add the liqueur, coffee or vanilla.

Bring the cream to the boil slowly in a heavy based saucepan, then pour cream over the chocolate. Let stand 30 seconds.

Gently stir the ganache (do not beat!) until smooth and glossy. Allow to cool until thick, then swirl over the cupcakes with a palette knife.

Makes 12 cupcakes

Note: These can be stored in an airtight container for 2-3 days – if they last that long. Gently reheat in a microwave for 15 seconds before serving. The chocolate in the centre melts, making them even moister.

Reader Viviane Buzzi

Polish babka

"My family is Polish, and for as long as I can remember mother baked a babka – a form of butter cake," says Peter Prysten. A dusting of icing sugar emphasises the swirls created by the special fluted tin, enhancing a moist, light cake with a lovely lemon flavour.

2 eggs

1 cup castor sugar

120g soft unsalted butter

1 tsp vanilla essence

finely grated rind of one lemon

2 cups self-raising flour

3/4 cup milk

2 dsstsp cocoa

Preheat oven to 190C.

Beat eggs and sugar until thick. Add butter, vanilla and lemon rind and beat well. Add flour and milk alternately. Keep beating until smooth.

Place half of mixture at the bottom of a well-greased and floured 6-cup babka tin. Add cocoa to the remaining mix and beat well. Pour over the vanilla mix in the tin and stir slightly to create swirls.

Bake for approximately 40 minutes. The cake is done when the top is firm to touch or a skewer inserted in the centre comes out clean.

Variation: For a fruity version, stir in 3/4 cup of sultanas after the flour and milk, and then pour mixture into tin.

Reader Peter Prysten

Very easy mini muffins

This simple recipe creates a moist, light-textured mouthful of
muffin — one is never enough!

1 cup cold water
1 cup sugar
125g butter
2 generous tbsp cocoa
¾ tsp bi-carb soda
2 eggs, beaten
1½ cups self-raising flour

Preheat oven to 180C.

Combine water, sugar, butter, cocoa and soda in a large saucepan.
Bring to the boil slowly. Simmer for 5 minutes and cool. Add eggs and
sifted flour and mix well. Place mixture in mini muffin trays. Cook for
10-15 minutes, or until the top springs back when pressed gently and
a toothpick inserted in the center comes out clean.

Cool slightly in pan and then remove to cooling rack.

Ice with chocolate ganache (see page 178).

Makes about 48 miniature muffins

Variation: This recipe also works well as a cake — use a 20cm babka
or ring tin and bake for 30-40 minutes.

Reader Anne Silverson

Daisie's German hazelnut cake

The chopped hazelnuts add texture to this wonderfully moist cake. "The recipe was given to me by my mother, Daisie, about 30 years ago," says Jennifer Rowe, a dedicated reader of Epicure since the very first issue in 1986. "It originally came to her from a German friend, a very skilled cook. I have made a few changes along the way. It's foolproof — it has even tolerated being forgotten in the oven for an extra 20 minutes!"

2 tbsp fine breadcrumbs
250g dark chocolate
200g butter
200g castor sugar
200g toasted hazelnuts, very finely chopped
6 eggs, separated
½ tsp cream of tartar
extra whole toasted hazelnuts, for decoration

Icing
2 cups pure icing sugar
1 tsp melted butter
2 tbsp espresso coffee (or 1 tsp
    of instant coffee dissolved in 2 tbsp
    boiling water)

Preheat oven to 170C.

Butter a 24cm round cake pan, line base with baking paper and shake breadcrumbs around pan to coat sides.

Melt chocolate, butter and sugar in a bowl over a saucepan of simmering water.

When sugar is dissolved, remove from heat, pour into a large bowl, stir hazelnuts through mixture and allow to cool for 10 minutes.

Add egg yolks, one at a time, beating in well with a fork.

Beat egg whites with cream of tartar until stiff.

Add about a cup of the beaten whites to chocolate nut mixture and stir through, then gently fold through the remainder.

Pour into cake pan and bake for about an hour or until the centre of cake feels firm.

Leave to cool in pan for 20 minutes before turning out. Cool completely before icing.

To make the icing: beat all ingredients together until smooth. Warm icing over hot water until it thins a little, if necessary, then spread over the cake. Decorate with toasted, whole hazelnuts or coffee beans.

Variations: If the recipient of the cake does not like coffee, Jennifer makes a chocolate icing by putting 125g chopped dark chocolate, 1 tablespoon Tia Maria or other liqueur and 60g butter into a bowl over hot water and stirring until the chocolate is melted and ingredients combined. Alternatively the cake can be served simply dusted with cocoa or icing sugar.

Reader Jennifer Rowe

Jaffa lamingtons

"My Aunty Pat was a great cook, known for her sponge cakes. When I was a child I gave her a battery-operated sifter which she good-naturedly used and claimed that it made her sponges ever lighter. I have used her sponge recipe here as the base for my lamingtons. Just bake the mix in a lamington tin. You won't believe how delicious these are – moist and light as a feather. And no battery-operated sifter required!"

1 sponge cake (see recipe below)
½ cup hot water
1 tbsp unsalted butter
2 tbsp Dutch cocoa
1 tbsp finely grated orange rind (optional)
1–2 tsp orange essence (optional)
2 cups icing sugar, sifted
2 cups desiccated coconut

Cut cake into small squares using a serrated knife. This is easier if the cake has been slightly chilled.

In a medium bowl, combine hot water, butter and cocoa and whisk until smooth. Add orange rind and essence at this point if you want jaffa-flavoured icing. (Traditionalists can ignore this step.)

Beat in icing sugar with a wooden spoon. Add extra hot water if the mixture is too thick for dipping. You want it quite runny, but still of a coating consistency.

Now for the messy bit. Place coconut in a tray or shallow bowl. Using two forks, dip the pieces of cake in the icing, one at a time, and turn them over to cover completely. Don't fuss too much about any errant crumbs. Now roll the cake in the coconut and place on a cake rack for the icing to set. It is a good idea to have a tray underneath to catch any drips. Repeat the process with the remaining cake. If your forks get too messy, just replace them with clean ones. Ditto, the coconut.

Store in an airtight container – if there are any left!

Auntie Pat's sponge

4 eggs, separated
¾ cup castor sugar
¾ cup cornflour
2 tsp self-raising flour
1½ tsp baking powder

Preheat oven to 200C.

Beat whites until stiff. Add castor sugar and mix in. Add yolks and mix. Sift cornflour, self-raising flour and baking powder and fold into mixture.

Pour into a greased and lined 22cm square lamington tin.

Bake for 20 minutes.

Epicure stylist Caroline Velik

Ellen the choc-malt cake

Why Ellen? "Because this simple, low-fuss cake is one you're going to want 'de Generes' slice of," says expat Melburnian Ben Johnson, who shares this and other crazy temptations at his website, thelovebite.com.

½ cup malted milk powder
⅓ cup cocoa
½ cup dark brown sugar
½ cup golden syrup
175g softened butter
1½ cups self-raising flour
½ tsp baking powder
2 eggs
⅔ cup buttermilk
¼ cup choc chips
Icing
150g dark chocolate
5 tbsp thickened cream
5 tbsp malted milk powder

Preheat oven to 200C. Grease and line a 22cm square baking dish (or equivalent).

Put all ingredients except for the choc chips into a food processor and pulse for 30 seconds. Scrape down the sides and add choc chips. Pulse for another 10 seconds.

Pour the batter into the dish. Bake for 10 minutes, reduce heat to 175C, then bake another 25 minutes. If cake bounces back when tapped in the centre, it is cooked.

Allow to cool in the baking dish for 10 minutes, run a knife around the edges to loosen then turn the cake onto a wire rack.

For the icing, melt the chocolate, mix the cream and malted milk powder to form a paste, then pour the melted chocolate into the bowl and stir to combine. Pour this over the cake and use a knife to spread it evenly.

Delicious served warm with ice-cream.

Reader Ben Johnson

Passover chocolate nut cake

8 eggs, separated
180g pure icing sugar, sifted
grated rind of one orange
90g dark chocolate, grated
75ml orange juice
1 tbsp sweet wine (Rutherglen muscat or tokay does nicely)
50g roasted hazelnuts, finely ground
75g blanched almonds, finely ground
70g fine matzah meal (see note)
2 tsp ground cinnamon
½ tsp ground mixed spice

Preheat oven to 170C. Grease a 25cm x 26cm springform tin.

Beat the yolks and icing sugar together until thick and pale, then fold in the grated orange rind, chocolate, orange juice, wine and nuts. Stir the matzah meal and spices together, then fold into the mixture. Beat the whites until stiff, and fold them, a quarter at a time, into the cake mixture.

Pour into tin and bake for about 45 minutes. Insert a toothpick into the centre of the cake to check whether it is done – if the toothpick is dry, the cake is ready. Allow to rest a few minutes before inverting the tin. Cool on rack.

Note: Matzah (or matzoh) meal is available in stores and supermarkets selling kosher food. It comes fine or coarsely ground, and I prefer fine ground for this. Grating chocolate can be tricky. I use the food processor, which leaves the chocolate slightly uneven, but that's fine. For the nuts, home-ground gives a better flavour than shop-ground, unless the shop grinds nuts daily.

Rita Erlich, Epicure editor 1992-94

Marion's applesauce cake

"I associate this cake with food parcels that arrived from home after I left the country for university in my late teens. In a big square cake tin, it became the standard manifestation of motherly love, delivered on or near my birthday," says Rod Duncan. "It is deliciously moist, courtesy of the stewed apples that are used instead of eggs. My mother based it on a recipe she heard on the wireless as a farm girl in 1939, and adapted over the years. She usually served it with a tangy lemon-juice-laden chocolate icing, studded with a crown of walnuts. It remains my favourite cake."

125g butter
1 cup sugar
1 tsp vanilla essence
2 tbsp cocoa
2 tsp baking soda
1½ cups warm stewed apples
2 cups self-raising flour
½ cup raisins
½ cup chopped walnuts
nutmeg to taste

Icing

2 cups icing sugar
2 tbsp cocoa
juice of one lemon
1 tsp melted butter
hot water
walnut halves, to decorate (optional)

Preheat oven to 180C. Grease a 22cm ring tin.

Cream butter and sugar, vanilla and cocoa. Add soda to apples and add to creamed butter, then add flour. Mix in raisins, walnuts and nutmeg.

Put batter into tin and spread evenly. Bake for 45 minutes or until a skewer comes out clean. Remove from oven and leave to cool for a few minutes. Turn out to cool.

To make icing, sift icing sugar and cocoa. Add lemon juice and butter with enough hot water to make a runny icing. Pour over cake and decorate with extra walnuts if, desired.

Reader Rod Duncan

Choc-chip banana muffins

Choc-chip banana muffins

1½ cups self-raising flour
½ cup brown sugar
150g chocolate chips
⅓ cup oil
1 egg
2 bananas, mashed
dash of vanilla essence
⅔ cups milk

Preheat oven to 180C.

Sift flour into a bowl. Add sugar and choc chips. Separately, mix oil and egg; add bananas, vanilla and milk and mix. Add to dry ingredients and mix until combined. Pour into greased muffin tray and bake for about 22 minutes.
Makes 12-14

Variation: Add 2 tablespoons of cocoa to increase the chocolate factor (sift in with the flour).

Reader Helen Gorman

Eggless chocolate cake

One might expect a recipe used during wartime – when eggs were scarce – to be a little Spartan. Not in this case. This recipe, which has been handed down in Kate Burke's family from her husband's step-grandmother, Elizabeth Glenn, makes a fantastic cake – soft and moist with a mouth-filling texture. It's not too sweet, either, so the cocoa flavour shines. The top of the cake is extra moist – almost like a built-in layer of icing. This is equally good served as a cake, or as a dessert with cream. Kate also uses the recipe for cupcakes.

100g butter
1 cup castor sugar
½ cup good-quality Dutch cocoa
1 jar SPC smooth apple sauce (or 375ml stewed apples)
2 cups plain flour
1 tbsp bicarb soda
¼ cup milk

Preheat oven to 165C. Grease a 20cm round cake tin.

Cream butter and sugar in a magimix or in a bowl with an electric beater. Add the cocoa and half of the apple and whiz or beat a few seconds. Add 1 cup flour and bicarb soda and mix in.

Add remaining apple, flour and milk; whiz to combine.

Place mixture in tin. Cook for one hour. Cool in tin a little before removing to cooling rack. Ice with chocolate butter frosting, if desired.

Variation: For cupcakes, grease a standard muffin tray (or line with pattie papers). Place mixture in tray and bake for 30-40 minutes at 160C.

Reader Kate Burke

"Best-ever" chocolate cake

"This has such a beautiful, deep, rich colour and a lovely firm but fluffy texture – something between a sponge and a not-too-dense mud cake. It's the jam in the batter that really makes it special," says Betty Penna. "I've been making it for 13 years now, for everyday eating and for children's birthday cakes, as it makes nice firmish slabs to cut into various shapes." She first found the recipe in a *Family Circle* recipe booklet, where the suggested topping was a butter cream, although Betty sometimes uses a chocolate ganache instead. Of course, there's always the option of no topping at all – this cake is so delicious, it would be just as good served plain.

125g butter
½ cup castor sugar
⅓ cup icing sugar
2 eggs, lightly beaten
1 tsp vanilla essence
¼ cup blackberry jam
1¼ cups self-raising flour, sifted
½ cup cocoa powder
1 tsp bicarb soda
1 cup milk

Chocolate Butter Cream
50g dark bitter chocolate, finely chopped
25g butter
3 tsp cream
¼ cup icing sugar, sifted

Ganache
⅔ cup cream
200g dark chocolate, chopped
⅓ cup castor sugar
1-2 tbsp of jam, melted

Preheat oven to 180C. Grease the base and sides of a deep 20cm square cake tin and line with baking paper.

In a large bowl, beat the butter and sugars with an electric beater until light and creamy. Add the eggs gradually, beating thoroughly between additions. Add the vanilla and jam and beat until combined.

Using a metal spoon, fold in the combined sifted flour, cocoa and bicarb soda alternately with the milk. Stir until the mixture is just combined and almost smooth.

Pour into the tin and smooth the surface. Bake for 45 minutes or until a skewer inserted in the middle comes out clean.

Leave in the tin for about 15 minutes then turn out onto a wire rack to cool.

For the butter cream, combine the chocolate, butter, cream and icing sugar in a small pan. Stir over a low heat until the mixture is smooth and glossy. Spread over the cake.

Alternatively, make a ganache by stirring the cream, chocolate and sugar over a low heat until the mixture melts and is smooth. Brush the melted jam over the cake and then top with the ganache. If the ganache is too runny, wait a few minutes, until it stiffens slightly, before using.

Variation: For a larger cake, Betty doubles the recipe, splits the cake in half and fills it with orange and cinnamon-spiced cream. Beat 600ml of cream until it just begins to thicken. Set aside. Melt 150g of white chocolate, allow to cool a little then fold into the cream. Chill, then flavor with grated orange rind and cinnamon and/or nutmeg to taste. Make this in advance if possible so the flavours have time to infuse.

Reader Betty Penna

This recipe is from Family Circle Classic Essential Chocolate, *and appears with the kind permission of the publishers,* Murdoch Books.

Queen of nuts cake

1 tbsp melted butter

2 tbsp fine breadcrumbs

100g best-quality dark chocolate, finely grated

150g blanched almonds, finely chopped

150g sugar

30g candied citron (or candied orange or lemon peel),
   cut into tiny cubes

5 egg yolks, lightly whisked with a drop of vanilla essence

5 egg whites

Preheat oven to 160C. Prepare a 22cm round tin (at least 5cm high) tin by brushing the inside with the melted butter and coating lightly with breadcrumbs.

Mix chocolate, almonds, sugar and citron. Stir in the yolks.

Beat the whites until they are satiny and in soft peaks. Gently fold into mix.

Bake for approximately 35 minutes until cake feels firm in centre. (A test skewer will still be moist because of the chocolate.) Cool in the tin for about 10 minutes before turning onto a cloth or foil-lined tray. Invert and allow to cool completely.

Serve dusted with icing sugar.

Food writer Stephanie Alexander, 1994

Chocolate Christmas cake

1¾ cups plain flour

pinch salt

1 tsp bicarb soda

1 tsp cinnamon

¼ tsp nutmeg

3 tbsp cocoa

125g unsalted butter

1 cup castor sugar

1 tsp vanilla essence

2 large eggs

⅓ cup milk

1 cup sultanas

½ cup mixed peel

½ cup chopped glacé cherries

¼ cup glacé ginger, chopped

½ cup coarsely grated dark chocolate or choc bits

some brandy

Preheat oven to 160C. Brush the base and sides of a square or round 20cm tin with melted butter and line the base with foil. Line the sides with nonstick baking paper and butter this as well.

Sift the flour with salt, bicarb soda, cinnamon, nutmeg and cocoa. Remove a half-cup of this so that it can be used to coat and separate the fruit.

Cream the butter and sugar with vanilla. Add eggs, one at a time. Mix in the flour alternately with the milk. Put all the fruit into a bowl with the chocolate and add the half-cup of flour. Stir so the fruits are coated and then mix them into the creamed batter, stirring well. Spoon this into the tin and smooth the top.

Bake for about 90 minutes or until the top is firm and a skewer in the centre emerges dry. This cakes firms as it cools.

Let it cool in the tin, then turn out and brush the top and sides with a little brandy. Wrap well and let mature for a couple of days before cutting.

Columnist Beverley Sutherland Smith, 1989

Omama's flourless chocolate cake

"My mother's chocolate cake has long been a favourite among our family and friends. Like my mother, the cake hails from Vienna (Omama is an affectionate term for a Viennese grandma). Not as rich as the famed Viennese sacher torte, but lighter, tastier and less fussy to prepare, this is best consumed with strong coffee and topped with whipped cream."

5 eggs, separated
115g castor sugar
115g dark cooking chocolate, melted
115g peeled, roasted ground hazelnuts (or hazelnut meal)
2 tbsp apricot jam
Chocolate glaze
40ml cream
80g dark cooking chocolate, melted

Preheat oven to 180C. Grease a 23cm loaf tin.

Place egg whites in mixer. Place on full power and beat to soft peak. Add sugar before proceeding to beat to a firm peak. Add cooled melted chocolate, eggs yolks and hazelnuts. Place processor on a moderate speed to combine (do not overmix). Pour into tin and bake for about 30 minutes. Remove and let cool.

Smear cake with a thin layer of apricot jam. Cover with glaze made from combined melted chocolate and cream.

Refrigerate.

Peter Weiniger, Epicure editor 1986-1988

Chocolate coconut cake

The Golden Rough of the cake world.

250g butter, melted
½ cup cocoa powder (a rich, dark Dutch cocoa powder is best for this)
1⅓ cups castor sugar
3 eggs
1½ cups desiccated coconut
1½ cups self-raising flour
¾ cup milk

Preheat oven to 180C.

Place the butter, cocoa powder, sugar, eggs, coconut, flour and milk into a bowl and mix until smooth.

Pour the mixture into a lined 24cm round-cake tin and bake for 50 minutes. Cool on a wire rack.

Spread the cake with chocolate icing if desired or serve with thick cream and a sprinkling of cocoa.

Columnist Donna Hay, 2001

Lisa's white chocolate cake

"This recipe is very adaptable and most importantly, NEVER fails," says Lisa O'Toole. "The texture is like a mud cake, but the recipe is so much easier."

½ cup (125ml) water
200g sugar
80g butter
100g white chocolate
2 eggs
100g self-raising flour, sifted
30g cocoa powder

Preheat oven to 190C. Grease a heart-shaped tin (about 20cm across) or a 20cm round tin and then line the base with baking paper.

Bring water to boiling point in a medium saucepan. Add the sugar and dissolve. Turn off the heat.

Add butter and chocolate, stir until melted. Cool slightly.

Beat eggs lightly and add to butter mix. Sift flour and cocoa powder into pan and mix well. Pour into prepared tin. Tap tin on bench to settle bubbles. Bake until done (about 30 minutes)

Cool in tin.

Ice with white chocolate ganache (see page 178).

Variations
1. Use 100g of milk or dark chocolate instead of the white chocolate.
2. For a caramel cake, add half a tin of Nestle Top'n'Fill Caramel at the melting stage instead of the chocolate – or leave in the chocolate for a caramello cake.
3. For a larger cake, the recipe multiplies well. However, Lisa suggests reducing the quantity of eggs to avoid an "eggy" taste – e.g. if making three times the mixture, use 5 eggs rather than 6.

Reader Lisa O'Toole

Fudgy family cake

This moist, easy-to-make cake has been a favourite of Jacki Getreu's family for many years. "The recipe was given to me by my aunt about 25 years ago, and she had been making it for years herself. I have changed it a little to cater for my family's liking for a fudgier cake — and I usually make a double batch because it is eaten so quickly!"

120g butter
1 x 250g block eating chocolate
2 cups self-raising flour
2 eggs
1½ cup sugar
¾ cup milk
½ cup warm water
½ cup cocoa
Icing
100g chocolate
100g butter
5 tsp warm water
3 tsp sugar
1 tsp vanilla essence

Preheat oven to 180C.

Melt chocolate and butter in a microwave dish on low for 1-2 minutes at a time, stirring after each minute to test for meltedness.

Mix all ingredients together by hand. Put mixture in a 20-22cm round tin. Bake for 45 minutes, then check. A little semi-cooked cake should be seen on a skewer inserted in the centre (this makes for an extra fudgy texture).

Cool on rack.

For icing, heat all ingredients together and mix. Use while warm.

Reader Jacki Getreu

Mississippi mud cake

Two readers sent us almost identical recipes for this dense, moist cake with a hint of coffee.

250g butter, chopped
150g dark chocolate, chopped
2 cups sugar (granulated or castor)
⅓ cup whisky
1 cup hot water
1 tbsp dry instant coffee
1½ cups plain flour
¼ cup self-raising flour
¼ cup cocoa
2 eggs, lightly beaten

Preheat oven to 150C. Grease a 23cm square cake tin; line base with baking paper and grease paper.

Combine butter, chocolate, sugar, whisky, water and coffee in a double saucepan or heatproof bowl. Stir over hot water until chocolate melts and mixture is smooth; cool to lukewarm.

Transfer mixture to large bowl, stir in sifted flours and cocoa, then eggs.

Pour into prepared pan. Bake for one and a quarter hours. (When this cake is cooked it may still look slightly underdone in the centre but will firm up as it cools. It will not pass the skewer test because of the melted chocolate it contains.)

Set aside for 10 minutes before turning onto wire rack to cool.

Serve dusted with sifted icing sugar, or as a dessert with thick cream and fresh strawberries.

Readers Marilyn Houghton and Margaret MacDonald

desserts105

Double-chocolate self-saucing puddings

100g butter, melted
½ cup milk
1 free-range egg
1 cup self-raising flour
1 tbsp cocoa
½ cup castor sugar
60g dark chocolate, roughly chopped
Topping
1 tbsp cocoa
1 cup firmly packed brown sugar
2 cups boiling water

Preheat oven to 180C.

In a large bowl, combine the butter, milk and egg. In a separate bowl, sift the flour and cocoa together, and mix in the sugar and chocolate. Gradually add the flour mixture to the wet ingredients and mix well. Spoon into four individual pudding bowls.

For the topping, combine the cocoa and sugar and sprinkle over the pudding mixture. Gently pour over the boiling water (half a cup per individual pudding). Cover the puddings with lids or foil and place on a baking tray (because the mixture might overflow). Bake for 30 minutes.

Serve immediately with lightly whipped cream.

Serves 4

Variation: This can also be made as one large pudding. Use the same ingredient quantities in a pudding bowl with a capacity of 1-1½ litres, and cook for about 45 minutes.

Columnist Luke Mangan, 2002

Savoiardi rum log

⅓ cup milk
¼ cup rum
1 packet Savoiardi (sponge finger) biscuits
150g unsalted butter
150g castor sugar
5 eggs, separated
100g dark chocolate
pinch of salt
whipped cream and grated chocolate, for decoration

Mix the milk and rum together in a cup. Line a 23cm loaf tin with the sponge finger biscuits, cutting them to fit both the bottom and sides of the tin. Reserve some for the top. Brush the biscuits with the rum mixture.

Beat the butter and sugar with an electric mixer until light and fluffy, then add the egg yolks one by one. Melt the chocolate and cool slightly. Add to egg mixture and stir to combine.

Beat egg whites with salt until stiff. Stir a couple of spoonfuls into the chocolate mixture, then fold in the rest gently. Put half the mixture into the loaf tin, scatter with any trimmings off the biscuits and top up with the rest of the chocolate mixture. Lay the rest of the sponge biscuits on top and brush with the remainder of the rum mix. Wrap the whole tin with foil and freeze for at least 24 hours. It can remain in the freezer for several days.

Remove from freezer one hour prior to serving. Remove wrapping and tip onto serving platter. Decorate with whipped cream and grated chocolate.

Reader Ida Maria Haigh

Chocolate brulee

A super-smooth, delicately flavoured chocolate custard under a thin, crisp toffee layer. Wicked and wonderful — and one of the best brulees the Epicure team has tried in years.

200ml milk
375ml cream
75g good quality chocolate buttons
    (or block chocolate cut into small pieces)
8 or 9 egg yolks (depending on the size of the eggs)
70g castor sugar
extra castor sugar, to serve

Bring milk and cream to the boil and add chocolate. Reduce heat and stir until the chocolate has melted completely. Remove from heat.

In a large bowl whisk together the yolks and the sugar until well combined.

Whisk the milk, cream and chocolate into the yolk mix.

Ensure all is well mixed together before straining through a fine chinois.

Pour into six 175ml ramekins and place in a bain marie tray with warm water reaching one third of the way up the sides.

Cover with foil and cook for 40-50 minutes. Check the water level during cooking. The brulees are ready when the mix has set to a firm custard (lightly shake the tray to check consistency).

Remove and allow to cool before placing in fridge to chill.

When serving, sprinkle layer of sugar on top and caramelise with blowtorch or under hot grill. Serve with ice-cream and orange cointreau syrup (see page 182).

Reader and chef Sonia Anthony

Tiramisu

"Tiramisu means 'pick me up' and is a classic Italian dessert that originated in my mother's home town of Treviso, north-east of Venezia," says Viviane Buzzi. "It's actually a fairly modern dessert, but has its roots an old, traditional pick-me-up treat that was given to children and adults alike whenever they needed to regain strength after an illness. I remember my grandmother used to beat a fresh egg with a little Marsala or espresso coffee." This creamy, alcoholic indulgence has a surprisingly light texture.

about 2 cups espresso coffee, freshly
    brewed (stove-top percolator is best)
3-4 tbsp brandy, cognac or liqueur,
    or to taste (see note)
300g fresh mascarpone
3 tbsp sugar
3 eggs, separated
12 large or 18 small savoiardi
    (sponge finger) biscuits
good-quality unsweetened cocoa or
    bittersweet chocolate, grated

Add the cognac, brandy or liqueur to the coffee. Leave to cool.

Beat the mascarpone, sugar and the egg yolks with an electric mixer on medium speed for about 15 minutes, until light. Beat the egg whites until stiff peaks form and very gently fold into the mascarpone mixture. It should have a texture like a rich mousse at this stage.

Dip the sponge fingers into the coffee until well soaked (otherwise you will have layers of dry biscuits) and make a layer of biscuits in a dish or on a serving plate (for example, about 6 biscuits side by side if using large savoiardi). Lift the biscuits carefully so they don't break. Follow with a layer of the mascarpone cream, then one of biscuits, and repeat until the cream is used up. The top layer should be mascarpone cream.

(To make a freestanding torte, make it with 2 layers of savoiardi and 2 layers of cream and use the any remaining cream to cover the sides of the tiramisu.)

Refrigerate for at least a few hours or overnight to allow the flavours to develop.

Before serving, sift some good quality unsweetened cocoa liberally over the top or cover the top with grated dark chocolate (a good quality couverture or one with at least 70 per cent cocoa solids).
Serves 6-8 as a dessert, but it can be easily doubled or tripled

Variation: Use 150g mascarpone and 150g King Island Double Cream. The flavour is not as "cheesy".

Note: If using a liqueur, pick something that marries well with coffee (Marsala, Grand Marnier, Amaretto or Frangelico are good). Plain old brandy works really well and is traditional.

Reader Viviane Buzzi

Jane's chocolate tart

"I serve this at most dinner parties – it's probably time I invented something new. But it is always devoured. It will serve about 10 (hungry) people."

Shortcrust pastry
240g plain flour, sifted
180g unsalted butter, roughly chopped
3 tbsp iced water

Chocolate filling
300ml thickened cream
1 tbsp castor sugar
100g unsalted butter
400g dark chocolate, roughly chopped
100ml milk

Preheat oven to 200C. Grease a 26cm non-stick loose-bottomed flan tin.

To make the pastry: on a cool piece of marble or bench top, place the sifted flour in a mound, add the chopped butter and start to combine by lightly rubbing together. Make a well in the centre of the mixture and add the water then use a pastry scraper to mix together or use the base of your hand. The pastry will start to come together even if it appears crumbly. When you can form a ball, dust with flour, wrap in plastic and refrigerate for at least 30 minutes. When ready, roll out pastry; try not to use too much flour and be light handed as the pastry is very delicate.

Use a rolling pin to lift pastry into tin. Don't worry if it breaks. Press down into the edges of the tin and patch up any thin bits – you don't want the chocolate topping to leak through. Chill the pastry for about 30 minutes before lining with foil and adding pastry weights or baking beans. Bake for about 15 minutes. Take the tart out, remove foil and pastry weights and return to the oven for 5-10 minutes to crisp slightly. Be careful not to overcook the pastry as it will shrink.

To make the filling, place the cream and sugar in a pan and bring to the boil. Take off the heat and immediately add the butter and chocolate, stirring until completely melted. Leave to cool slightly before whisking in the milk. Place the mixture in a jug and slowly pour the chocolate through a sieve into the still-warm tart shell. Leave to set in a cool spot (don't refrigerate). The tart will have a beautiful sheen, too lovely to mask with any topping, so just serve as is on a plate with some berries and a touch of cream.

If there's filling left over, refrigerate to use as a topping for ice-cream.

Age journalist Jane Faulkner

Chocolate and Turkish coffee sorbet

Chocolate and Turkish coffee sorbet

"This beautiful and exotic sorbet comes from my time working with Melbourne chef Greg Malouf."

1 heaped tbsp Turkish coffee, finely ground (see note)
¾ cup boiling water
1275ml water
375g castor sugar
150g liquid glucose (see note)
3 cardamom pods, cracked open
100g Dutch cocoa powder

Pour boiling water over the coffee, allow to infuse for a few minutes then pour into a pot through muslin cloth or a very fine sieve. Add the extra 1275ml water, sugar, glucose, cardamom pods and cocoa powder.

Gently bring to the boil, whisking until combined and simmer for 5 minutes. Strain through a fine strainer and pour into a cold bowl. Cool completely before churning in an ice-cream maker. Alternatively, pour into a flat tray and freeze. Every half hour or so, remove from freezer and break up with a fork. Repeat until completely frozen (about 2 hours).

Note: Turkish coffee is more finely ground than normal coffee. Liquid glucose can be bought at health food stores.

Columnist Brigitte Hafner, 2005

So-easy ice-cream

"It looks as though you are very talented – and tastes terrific," says Marie Brennan of this dessert, which even those who never cook should find a breeze.

2L good vanilla ice-cream
1 x 100g block toblerone chocolate, crushed or chopped
melted chocolate – as much as you like (or use an instant chocolate topping such as Ice Magic)
1 x 425g tin or similar-sized bottle of berries or cherries

Chill tin of fruit in refrigerator. Defrost ice-cream just enough so you can stir in the crushed Toblerone. Place ice-cream mixture in a springform pan and return to freezer to set.

To serve, remove from springform, swirl on chocolate and pour on fruit.

Variation: Add toasted flaked or slivered almonds to the ice-cream along with the Toblerone.

Reader Marian Brennan

Chocolate royal torte

Very rich, yet light and airy to eat, with an intriguing hint of cinnamon.

Meringue shell
4 egg whites
pinch of salt
1½ cups sugar
1 tsp cinnamon
1 tsp vinegar

Filling
175g semi-sweet chocolate
4 egg yolks
½ cup water
250ml cream
¼ cup sugar
½ tsp cinnamon

nuts or chocolate shavings, for decoration

Preheat oven to 135C. Cover an oven tray with a sheet of baking paper and draw a 20cm circle in the middle.

Whip egg whites with salt to stiff peaks. Gradually beat in half the sugar, adding it to the mixture one tablespoon at a time. Fold in the remaining sugar with the cinnamon and vinegar.

Spread the meringue mixture within the circle drawn on the baking paper, making the bottom 2cm thick. Mound the remainder of the mixture around the edges, making it about 5cm high. Bake for 1-1¼ hours or until meringue has set.

For the filling, melt the chocolate over hot water. Cool slightly and spread three tablespoons of the chocolate on the bottom of the cooked and cooled meringue shell.

To the remaining chocolate, add egg yolks and water. Blend well, and cook over hot water until it thickens into a custard. Chill.

Combine the cream, sugar and cinnamon and whip until thick. Spread half over the chocolate in the shell, and fold the remainder into the chocolate custard mixture, which is then spread on top.

Chill for several hours or overnight. Trim the top with a little more whipped cream if desired and decorate with nuts or chocolate shavings.

Reader Decima Frazer

Chocolate gateau with raspberry brulee

Chocolate sponge

4 x 55g eggs

100g castor sugar

130g self-raising flour

25g cocoa

Raspberry brulee palette

125ml milk

125ml cream (35 per cent fat)

50g castor sugar

4 egg yolks

100g fresh or frozen raspberries

Chocolate mousse

200g dark couverture chocolate

100g castor sugar

80ml water

3 egg yolks

1 x 55g egg

300ml cream (35 per cent fat), softly whipped

Garnish

chocolate curls or shavings (to taste)

extra raspberries (to taste)

Preheat oven to 180C.

To make the sponge: whisk the eggs and sugar until thick and pale. Sieve the flour and cocoa together and carefully fold through the egg base. Transfer to a buttered and floured 20cm cake tin. Bake for 30 minutes. Remove.

Reduce heat to 110C.

To make the palette: bring milk and cream to boiling point on a high heat. Combine the sugar and yolks in a bowl and add the boiled ingredients, stirring well to combine. Transfer into an 18cm cake tin that has been lined with plastic film. Scatter half the raspberries over the mixture and bake for one hour. Cool in the tin then transfer to the freezer to solidify for about two hours or overnight.

To make the chocolate mousse: melt chocolate in a double saucepan or microwave and cool. Set aside. Combine the sugar and water. Bring to boil on a high heat and cook to 120C (soft ball stage). Meanwhile, whisk the egg yolks and the egg until pale, carefully pour in the cooked sugar and continue whisking

until cool. Using a hand-held whisk, swiftly combine the melted chocolate with the egg mix, then add in the softly whipped cream. Mix only until combined.

To assemble: place a 20cm ring on a serving plate. Slice the chocolate sponge into three pieces horizontally. Start with one layer of sponge. Lightly brush it with sugar syrup (made with a mix of 250ml water and 200g castor sugar). Spoon in one-third of the chocolate mousse, scatter remaining raspberries on top. Position the second layer of sponge and brush that with syrup. Spoon in chocolate mousse to form another layer. Onto this, position the frozen brulee palette after removing the plastic film. Position the third layer of sponge, brush with syrup and flood surface with the remaining chocolate mousse. Refrigerate for at least three hours. To serve, garnish with chocolate curls or shavings and extra raspberries.

Pastry chef Loretta Sartori, 1990

Hazelnut chocolate torte

Embracing the spirit of a book that looks back over decades of trends and change, Gayle Austin shares a recipe that was a huge hit in the 1970s. "I used to make it for all my dinner parties!" It's smooth, rich and chocolatey – make it with good-quality chocolate for a retro-groovy dessert.

½ cup hazelnuts, plus extra for decoration
250g dark chocolate
4 eggs, beaten
200g copha
1 x 250g pkt Nice biscuits

Preheat oven to 180C.

Spread nuts on tray in and toast until golden brown. Remove from oven and rub in tea towel to remove skins. Measure 1/2 cup and chop finely.

Line a 22cm x 7cm loaf tin with foil. Melt chocolate over hot water, lightly stirring occasionally. Cool a little. Gradually stir in eggs and chopped nuts.

Melt copha over gentle heat and stir into chocolate one teaspoon at a time.

Pour a layer into the tin, about half a centimetre deep. Cover with layer of biscuits, trimming to fit. Continue layering till all mixture is used, finishing with chocolate. Chill to set.

Turn out, peel off foil and decorate with extra toasted hazelnuts. Serve with cream.

Gayle Austen, Epicure editor 1989-1991

Chocolate cream

250g good quality milk chocolate
6 eggs, separated
600ml cream, whipped
a few drops of vanilla essence

Melt chocolate in a double saucepan or in a large basin over hot water.

Remove from heat. Add egg yolks one at a time, beating well. (If the mixture is too stiff at this stage, add a little cream.

Mix in whipped cream and few drops of vanilla.

Whip egg whites and fold in.

Spoon into glasses or bowls and refrigerate.

Reader Sarah Simcock

Chocolate date torte

3 egg whites
½ cup castor sugar
115g almonds, very finely chopped
115g dates, finely chopped
115g dark chocolate, grated
whipped cream

Preheat oven to 180C. Grease a 22-23cm springform tin and line with aluminium foil.

Beat egg whites until soft peaks form. Gradually beat in sugar; beat until dissolved.

Fold in almonds, dates and chocolate. Pour into tin.

Bake for 35-40 minutes. Cool in tin.

To serve, top with whipped cream.

Age journalist Kirsty Simpson

Layered chocolate mousse

This stylish dessert wins votes for taste, too — it has a lovely, lightly set texture and is not too sweet.

800ml cream
4 eggs
250g white chocolate
250g dark chocolate
2 tsp gelatine
2 tbsp boiling water

Beat 400ml cream until semi-whipped. Set aside.

Crack 2 eggs into a stainless-steel bowl. Sit the bowl over a saucepan of gently simmering water and whisk until the eggs turn pale and frothy (about 2 minutes).

Meanwhile, melt the white chocolate in a small saucepan or microwave. Dissolve 1 teaspoon of the gelatine in 1 tablespoon of boiling water, stirring well.

Pour a third of the egg mixture into the chocolate and mix well, then stir through the remaining egg mixture. Add to the semi-whipped cream and stir through the dissolved gelatine, mixing until well combined.

Place in a large bowl and refrigerate.

Make a dark chocolate mousse by repeating the process with remaining ingredients.

Refrigerate both mousses for about three hours. Remove from the fridge. In serving glasses, spoon a layer of dark chocolate mousse, then a layer of white chocolate mousse and so on. Return to fridge to set for several more hours or overnight.
Makes 8

Columnist Luke Mangan

Fig and chocolate tart

Tart crust

¼ cup icing sugar

1½ cups plain flour

150g butter, chopped

1 egg yolk, beaten

iced water

Chocolate almond filling

185g butter

¾ cup castor sugar

30g plain flour

185g ground almonds

3 eggs, beaten lightly

150g dark cooking chocolate, melted and cooled

6 ripe figs

extra cooking chocolate (you will need
    12 x 1cm squares)

icing sugar, for dusting

To make the crust, stir the icing sugar into the flour in a large bowl. Add the butter and work in with a fork, until the mixture resembles breadcrumbs. Add the egg yolk and enough iced water so that the mix just comes together. Form into a ball, cover with plastic wrap and refrigerate until well chilled. (Alternatively, the tart crust can be made in a food processor, according to processor directions).

Preheat oven to 180C.

Remove pastry from refrigerator, roll out and use to line a deep 23-25cm tart tin with removable base. Cover pastry with greased foil or baking paper, and fill with dried beans or similar. Bake for 15 minutes. Remove paper and beans, and cook 5 minutes more to help dry base. Remove and cool. Reduce heat to 160C.

For the filling, cream butter and sugar until smooth. Add flour and ground almonds and mix well. Add the beaten eggs slowly, blending well, then stir in melted chocolate. Spoon into prepared tart crust.

Cut any stalks from figs and split in two. Place a piece of chocolate in the middle of each fig half. Place the fig halves on the surface of the chocolate almond filling, cut side up, and gently press in.

Place the tart tin on a large baking tray with turned up edges (to catch any over-run if figs are very ripe). Bake until the filling is firm to the touch (30-45 minutes), taking care not to scorch the tart crust. If the crust begins to darken, lower the heat and continue cooking. Remove from oven and place on cake rack for 10 minutes, then lift out of tin. Sift icing sugar over surface before serving. The tart can be served warm with cream, or cold with vanilla or chocolate ice-cream.

Reader Margaret Cornish

"Chocolate is one of life's luxuries ... my favourite chocolate experiences all tend to centre around bitter, very dark chocolate – the more bitter the chocolate the more intense the flavour. I especially like it paired with roasted almonds, deep caramel or orange peels. The perfect choice for cakes, puddings and sauces, too."

Stephanie Alexander

White chocolate, macadamia and butterscotch tart

Alex Roser – then chef and co-owner at Carlton's Arc Cafe, now cooking on Victoria's Mornington Peninsula – shared this recipe some years ago in an Epicure column called Ask The Chef. The macadamias and coconut help to balance the intensely rich, sweet, fudgy filling. For best results, use really fresh nuts.

Pastry

250g plain flour

100g icing sugar

100g unsalted butter, chilled and
    cut into 2cm cubes

1 egg, chilled

1 egg yolk

Filling

2¼ cups macadamia nuts

3 cups shredded coconut

4 cups cream

2 cups brown sugar

1 vanilla bean

2 cups white Belgian chocolate buttons

To make pastry: in a blender, blend the flour, sugar and butter until the mixture resembles breadcrumbs. Add the egg and extra yolk, and blend at high speed until it forms a dough. Rest the dough in the fridge overnight, or for at least two hours, wrapped in plastic wrap.

You will need a 32cm flan tin with a detachable base. This does not need to be greased.

On a floured board, roll the pastry out until it is large enough to line the tin all the way up the sides. Roll the pastry round a rolling pin and unroll it into the tin. Prick the pastry case in several places with a fork. Freeze the case for at least an hour, or until required. It will keep for up to a fortnight in the freezer.

Preheat oven to 180C.

Bake case for 20-30 minutes. The pastry should be just cooked and a very light golden brown. It can be baked straight from the freezer.

For the filling, spread the macadamia nuts and the coconut on separate trays. Roast for 12-15 minutes, until the nuts are golden brown and the coconut is golden. The nuts should be stirred every three to four minutes, and the coconut every couple of minutes. Watch carefully to ensure they don't burn.

Put the cream and sugar in a pan. Cut the vanilla bean lengthways and scrape the seeds into the mixture. Drop the bean in as well, but remove it before filling the flan. Bring liquid to the boil and simmer, stirring constantly with a wooden spoon until the mixture reduces by half (about 30 minutes). Set aside in a large bowl and allow to cool.

When cool, add the chocolate, nuts and two cups of the coconut and mix through gently. (For just the right texture, it's important to mix the chocolate, nuts and coconut in as soon as the fudge is cool to touch; don't let it get chilled before it goes in the flan.)

Pour the mixture into the flan case, smooth over with a wet knife and sprinkle the remaining coconut on top. Refrigerate for an hour and serve with thick cream. The tart should set to a firm but soft consistency resembling fudge.

Chef Alex Roser, 1998

Chocolate bread & butter pudding

Chocolate bread & butter pudding

Lemon-scented custard soaks through the bread and contrasts with the oozing richness of the melting choc bits and crunchy walnuts in this version of the classic dessert.

50g butter

2 eggs + 2 egg yolks

100g castor sugar

400ml milk

200ml cream

rind of one lemon

8 slices stale white bread

2 handfuls walnuts, roughly chopped

100g dark chocolate, broken in pieces

Preheat oven to 175C. Grease a 20cm x 30cm baking dish with half the butter.

Cream eggs and yolks with sugar. Mix in milk and cream, then add lemon rind.

Put 4 slices of bread in baking dish. Pour over half the egg mixture. Sprinkle with the walnuts and chocolate. Cover with the other 4 slices of bread. Pour over remaining egg mixture and dot with butter. Put in the oven and bake for 30 minutes.

Note: A sprinkle of brown sugar (2-3 tablespoons) over the top before the dish goes in the oven adds a little crunch and a lovely caramel note.

Reader Agnes Girdwood

Chocolate fudge pudding

"This is covered in so much cocoa and flour that it is difficult to read," said Heather Mabilia when she sent Epicure this recipe. "I grew up on a dairy farm and learnt to cook at an early age. As Mum worked in the shed helping Dad milk cows every afternoon, my sisters and I had to help cook. We used to make double the recipe of this chocolate pudding so we could have bigger helpings!" This is a very fudgy, moist pudding with lots of chocolate sauce underneath.

1 cup self-raising flour

½ tsp salt

2 tbsp cocoa

¾ cup brown sugar

¾ cup milk

2 tbsp butter, melted

½ tsp vanilla essence

⅓ cup chopped nuts

Topping

¾ cup brown sugar

2 tbsp cocoa

1¾ cups boiling water

Preheat oven to 180C.

Sift flour, salt and cocoa together, add sugar and beat in milk, butter and vanilla. Mix in nuts. Pour into ovenproof pie dish or pudding basin or a 20cm round cake tin.

Mix topping ingredients together and pour over main mixture, completely covering the pudding. Bake for 50-60 minutes (Do not overcook or the sauce will dry out).

Serve with cream.

Reader Heather Mabilia

This recipe first appeared in a Calendar of Puddings published many years ago by the the South Australian Country Women's Association Inc. and appears with the kind permission of the association.

Chocolate mud-cups

This rich, creamy and stylish dessert is so, so simple to make.

600ml thickened cream
300g good-quality dark chocolate buttons (e.g. Callebaut)
2 level tbsp instant coffee granules
1 vanilla bean, seeds scraped (save pod for use in a vanilla sugar canister)
½ cup pure cream, for decoration
2 tsp sifted cocoa

Pour cream into microwave-safe glass jug and heat on high for
3 minutes. Add other ingredients. Let sit for 4 minutes, then use
Bamix or similar utensil and blend until smooth.

Pour into small espresso cups. Chill in fridge for at least 4 hours.
When ready to serve, place cups on saucers, dollop a teaspoon of
cream on top and sprinkle with sifted cocoa.

Reader Theone Snow

Walnut-filled pancakes with chocolate sauce

A delicious and completely decadent dessert based on an old recipe from a famous restaurant in Budapest, now more than a century old, called Gundel's. The filling can be made ahead of time, but it's best to make the pancakes on the day and the sauce at the last minute.

Pancakes

3 eggs, beaten

1 cup milk

1 cup plain flour

50g butter

Filling

125g walnuts

60g raisins

60g sugar

zest of half a lemon

4 tbsp dark rum or brandy

Sauce

3 tbsp Dutch cocoa

3 tbsp sugar

3 yolks

200ml milk

100ml cream

125g dark chocolate, chopped

4 tbsp dark rum or brandy

60g butter, to finish cooking pancakes

extra rum, to serve

To make the pancakes, whisk the eggs and milk into the flour until you have a smooth batter. Let stand for 10 minutes. The consistency should be like pouring cream – you may need to add a touch more milk.

Heat a frying pan and add a knob of butter and move it around so that it covers the pan. When the butter is foaming, pour in a ladle of batter (about half a cup), moving the pan around so that the batter covers the whole bottom. Cook over a medium high heat until the pancake is golden brown underneath. Turn and cook the other side then transfer to a plate. Continue with the rest of the batter.

For the filling, finely chop the walnuts (or blitz in a food processor) and the raisins and combine with the sugar, zest and rum. Place a spoonful on each pancake and fold into four so that they look like triangles.

For the sauce, beat the cocoa, sugar and yolks together. Bring the milk and cream to the boil and pour over the yolks, whisking. Return to the heat and cook gently, stirring, until the custard thickens. Remove from heat and add the chocolate and rum, stirring until combined. Keep warm while cooking the pancakes.

To finish, heat a large frying pan with the butter and add the filled pancakes, frying gently to warm them through. Cook on both sides.

Sprinkle a little extra rum over the pancakes and serve them immediately with the chocolate sauce poured over the top.
Serves 4-6

Columnist Brigitte Hafner, 2006

Ricotta and praline cake

Nine years ago, after a reader begged for it to be included in Epicure's 'Ask The Chef' column, cake maker Julie Campbell agreed to share her recipe for this soft, cheesecake-like dessert. The Nudel Bar, where the cake was originally made, has generously allowed its publication here.

Crumb crust
1 cup self-raising flour
2 cups plain flour
1 cup almond meal
¾ cup brown sugar
250g soft butter, cubed
1 55g egg

Filling
750g ricotta cheese
1 cup castor sugar
2 tsp vanilla essence
70g dark chocolate, coarsely grated
praline, finely ground

Praline
½ cup castor sugar
4 tbsp pine nuts, toasted

Preheat oven to 190C. Grease and line a 28cm springform cake tin.

To make crust: sift flours into a large mixing bowl. Add almond meal and sugar and mix roughly. Pour into food processor and blend in butter a few pieces at a time. Add egg and mix until fine and crumbly. (If you do not have a food processor, mix in a bowl with a wooden spoon.)

Divide the crumb-crust mixture in half and put aside. It should be crumbly but should form a ball in the hands when pressed together.

To make praline: heat sugar gently over low heat until it melts and turns pale gold. Stir in toasted pine nuts and cook slowly, stirring frequently, on a low heat until mixture forms a pale gold toffee. While still hot, pour onto a sheet of baking paper and leave to set. When cool, smash the sheet of praline into chunks and whiz in a food processor or pound with a meat mallet until it has is the texture of breadcrumbs.

To make the filling: cream the ricotta cheese with the sugar in a large mixing bowl. Add vanilla essence, grated dark chocolate and ground praline and beat until well mixed.

Press half the crumb crust mixture firmly into tin. Pour in the filling. Gently press the remaining crust over the top.

Bake in centre of oven for about 70 minutes, or until firm to the touch and golden brown in the centre. Rotate the cake half-way through cooking (many ovens are hotter at the back than at the front).

Remove from oven and allow to cool. When cold, invert cake to give smoother surface, dust with icing sugar and serve (still inverted) with a spoonful of King Island cream.

The cake will keep well for 4-5 days in the refrigerator.

The Nudel Bar team, 1997

Chocolate Boston cream pie

"Boston cream pie — actually a cake, not a true pie — is a traditional American recipe," says Margaret Cornish, who first came across it while living in America in the '70s and later developed this version for her family. A big, delicious layered treat filled with creamy vanilla custard and topped with rich dark choc icing, it can be served as dessert or a cake. The custard layer can be made in advance and the cake assembled when needed.

125g shortening, at room temperature

1½ cups castor sugar

2 large eggs

¼ cup cocoa (preferably Dutch)

1½ tsp vanilla essence (real)

1½ cups plain flour

¾ cup self-raising flour

1½ tsp baking powder

¼ tsp salt

¾ cup milk

Vanilla filling

3 egg yolks (from large eggs)

¼ cup sugar

2 tbsp plain flour

250ml milk

2 tsp vanilla essence

Chocolate glaze

200g dark cooking chocolate

60g butter

Preheat oven to 160C. Grease a 25cm metal pie tin or springform tin (if using a loose-bottomed tin, line completely with greased foil).

Cream shortening and sugar. Add eggs one at a time and beat until smooth. Beat in cocoa and vanilla. Add the flours, baking powder and salt, alternately with milk. Spread batter evenly in prepared tin. Bake for 30-40 minutes, or until the top springs back when lightly pressed with fingertips. Cool in tin for 10 minutes, then loosen and invert onto a rack. When completely cool, split into halves horizontally.

For the vanilla filling, whisk the egg yolks and half the sugar until a pale lemon colour. Sift in the flour and mix in well. Place the milk, remaining sugar and vanilla essence in a saucepan and bring to boil. As soon as milk starts to bubble, quickly lift off heat and pour about one third onto the egg mix, stirring continuously until blended. Pour this mixture back into the saucepan, and continue to stir over low heat. Cook until the mixture thickens.

Pour into a bowl and cover the surface with plastic wrap to prevent a skin forming. Refrigerate until needed.

For the chocolate glaze, chop chocolate and butter into small, even-sized pieces. Place in heatproof bowl over a saucepan of water that has been brought to the boil, then lifted off the heat. Make sure that the bowl does not touch the water and that steam does not rise into the chocolate and butter. Stir gently until smooth. Alternatively, melt in microwave, according to oven instructions.

To assemble, place one half on a large serving plate, and top with vanilla filling (if the cake has been baked in a pie tin, one half will be larger — use this as the base). Carefully place the other half on top. Spread with chocolate mixture. Serve in wedges as cake or dessert.

Reader Margaret Cornish

Indulgence cheesecake

This rich dessert, stylish could just as easily be called Cheesecake of Many Faces. Helen Robb developed her recipe about 30 years ago, and has been making variations of it ever since.

Base
250g packet chocolate ripple biscuits, crushed
125g melted butter
1 tbsp walnuts, hazelnuts or other nuts,
    finely chopped
1 tbsp melted dark chocolate, melted
Filling
1 tbsp gelatine
½ cup strong brewed coffee
250g cream cheese
395g tin condensed milk
125-250g good quality dark chocolate
1 tsp vanilla essence or add your favourite liqueur to taste (optional)
1 cup cream

For the base, mix crushed biscuits with other ingredients and press into base and halfway up sides of 20cm springform tin. Chill while making the filling.

For filling, dissolve gelatine in hot coffee, cool. Beat cream cheese until soft. Beat in condensed milk, then beat in gelatine mixture, chocolate and vanilla or flavouring. Beat cream until thick, then stir into the mixture.

Pour into prepared tin and chill overnight. To serve, top with whipped cream and anything you fancy, such as berries or chocolate curls.

Variations: As an alternative base, use 250g plain sweet biscuits in place of the ripple biscuits. Make as instructed above, using a teaspoon of honey in place of the chopped nuts. Rum-soaked cherries, prunes or fresh dates make an interesting addition folded through the filling. For a very rich version, omit the biscuit shell and line a foil-lined springform tin with melted chocolate. Set before adding filling. Peel foil off the next day when it's well set and decorate the top with chocolate leaves.

Reader Heather Robb

Choc-mint ice-cream

A creamy ice-cream without the need for an ice-cream maker.

¾ cup castor sugar
1 cup of water
500g dark couverture chocolate chips
1-2 tbsp peppermint essence
8 egg yolks
1 litre thickened cream

Place the sugar and water in a small saucepan and gently heat until the sugar has dissolved. Bring to the boil then remove from the heat. Add the chocolate and mix until smooth. Add peppermint essence to taste. Set aside to cool.

Beat egg yolks in a clean bowl and slowly add to cooled chocolate mixture.

Whip cream until soft peaks form.

Fold the chocolate mixture into the cream. You can add chunks of peppermint chocolate at this stage, if desired.

Pour mixture into a suitable container, cover with cling wrap and freeze until set – approximately 2-3 hours.

Transfer to the refrigerator for about half an hour before serving to allow it to soften slightly.
Makes 2 litres

Epicure stylist Caroline Velik

Chocolate blini

This dessert is a favourite with diners at the European restaurant in Melbourne. Break through the crust to reveal a moist, gooey middle.

250g unsalted butter, chopped
250g dark chocolate
5 whole eggs
5 egg yolks
125g castor sugar
70g plain flour, sifted
3 egg whites

Preheat oven to 180C.
   Place the butter and chocolate in a large stainless-steel bowl. Place on top of a pot of boiled water away from the heat source.
   In a kitchen mixer bowl, cream together the 5 whole eggs and 5 yolks with the castor sugar until the mixture is light and pale. Fold through the flour.
   Beat the egg whites until stiff. Pour melted chocolate and butter mixture into egg and flour mixture and mix, and then fold through the stiff egg whites.
   Ladle completed batter into cast iron blini pans (see note) and bake for 12 minutes. Serve with cream and fruit (at the European it is served with vanilla bean-scented cream, brandy spiked sour cherries and Valrhona chocolate sorbet.)
   The uncooked batter can be refrigerated in the blini pans for up to 3 days.
Makes 10-12

Note: The blini pans used for this recipe are about 10cm across and about 1.5cm deep. They are available from some specialist kitchenware/chef's supplies retailers. As an alternative, small flat ovenproof terracotta dishes could be used. Look for dishes about 10cm in diameter and no deeper than 2.5cm.

Kyle Doody, head chef, European, Melbourne

Chocolate and raspberry pudding

Andrew Stephens has shared his passion for pies, puddings, cakes and other home-baked treats in Epicure many times, including this recipe for a pudding crowned with berry sauce.

115g soft butter

115g sugar

2 eggs

115g plain flour

1 tsp baking powder

2 heaped tbsp of cocoa

1 tbsp milk

100g raspberries (defrosted from frozen or fresh)

50g dark chocolate, broken into small chips or grated

Sauce

2 tbsp raspberry jam

½ cup water

100g raspberries (frozen or fresh)

1 tsp cornflour dissolved in a little cold water

Cream butter and sugar with an electric beater, then add eggs one at a time until blended. Sift in flour, baking powder and cocoa and mix until smooth. Mix in the milk and then stir through the raspberries and chocolate. The mixture is quite thick. Put in greased pudding mould, seal and steam for two hours in a saucepan with water halfway up the mould. Continue to maintain water level. Allow to cool for 10 minutes before unmoulding.

To make sauce: stir jam into water and bring to the boil. Add the fruit and simmer, stirring, for 3 minutes. Stir in the cornflour until mixture thickens. Serve hot over the pudding, with thick cream.
Serves 8-10

Age journalist Andrew Stephens

Chocolate souffle puddings

Lighter than a pudding and richer than a souffle, this combines the best of both.

1 tsp butter

150g bittersweet chocolate, chopped

85g castor sugar

1 tbsp brandy, rum or whisky

½ tsp vanilla essence

4 large eggs, separated

1 tbsp plain flour, sifted

Preheat oven to 190C. Butter four 150ml heatproof souffle bowls or ramekins and place on a baking tray.

Melt the chopped chocolate in a heatproof bowl set over a pot of gently simmering water.

Remove from the pot, allow to cool slightly, then beat in the castor sugar, brandy and vanilla essence. Beat in the egg yolks, one by one, and then the flour. The mixture will be fairly stiff.

Whisk or beat the egg whites until stiff and peaky, then gently fold them into the chocolate mixture.

Pour into the prepared pots and bake for 10-12 minutes until well-risen. They should still be a little gooey inside.

The puddings can be baked earlier, and reheated at 190C for a further 10 minutes. They will rise again by about two-thirds their original height, and be gooey and pudding-like inside.
Serves 4

Food writer Jill Dupleix, 2000

Chocolate souffle puddings

Semifreddo di Cioccolata

This smooth, rich semifreddo is easy to make as it doesn't require an ice-cream churn and never sets hard. Just pour it into a mould and wait for it to set in the freezer.

200g dark couverture or good quality chocolate
　　(with at least 70 per cent cacao solids)
150g sugar
50ml water
4 eggs, separated
500ml double cream, cold (see note)
1-2 tbsp flavouring (liqueur, grated orange rind,
　　vanilla essence etc), optional

Chop the chocolate and melt in a heatproof bowl over hot water (or in a microwave). Stir gently until smooth. Set aside to cool slightly. Dissolve the sugar and water over a low heat. Bring gently to the boil until a syrup forms. Do not allow to caramelise. Pour onto beaten egg yolks, beating well until the mixture is light and forms a thick ribbon. This can take up to 15 minutes.

Gently fold the chocolate into the egg yolk mixture. Leave to cool. Whisk the cream until soft peaks form. At this point, add the flavouring of your choice, if desired. Fold the egg mixture very gently into the cream. Beat the egg whites until stiff peaks form. Gently fold the whites into the yolk-cream mixture. Pour into a one-litre mould lined with cling film. Leave the cling film hanging over the sides so it can be used to ease out the semifreddo when set. Place in the freezer and allow to set for several hours or overnight. It is best made several hours and up to a day in advance so as to allow flavours to develop, especially if adding liqueurs, vanilla etc.

To serve, turn out of mould onto a serving dish. Slice the semifreddo and place onto plates. Serve with seasonal fruit, chocolate sauce and/or wafers or delicate biscuits.
Serves 6-8

Note: Do not use thickened cream for this. You really want to use double (heavy) cream that has 48-50 per cent fat. Whip it gently by hand, using a whisk. If you use an electric beater, it can easily separate and turn to butter.

Reader Viviane Buzzi

Chocolate croissant cake

Epicure readers still write in asking for a copy of this recipe, first published 10 years ago when Chef Colin Masters, then at Melbourne's Hydrometer's Cafe, shared the recipe for his twist on the traditional bread and butter pudding. Masters, now chef and co-owner at the Brunswick Green, put it on the menu there this year. "It was still as popular as ever."

6 large croissants
1 cup dark chocolate, grated
10 x 55g eggs
250g castor sugar
a few drops of vanilla essence
800ml full-cream milk
250ml thickened cream

Preheat oven to 170C. Grease a 25cm springform tin.

Split croissants lengthways and fill them with about three quarters of the grated chocolate. Place filled croissants in two layers across the base of the tin.

Whisk eggs, sugar and vanilla essence in a stainless-steel bowl. Bring milk and cream to the boil in a saucepan, stirring frequently. Whisking rapidly, add the hot liquid to the egg mixture a little at a time. Pour mixture over the croissants. Gently press the croissants down into the mixture until most of the air is expelled. Sprinkle remaining chocolate over the top.

Bake for 30-45 minutes (depending on the efficiency of the oven) or until it is firm to the touch and set, but not hard, and a chocolate brown color on top.

Cool for up to an hour in the tin. Dust top with icing sugar and serve warm in wedges with pouring cream. (Reheat cut wedges if necessary.)
Serves 8

Variation: Epicure reader Noela Lynch makes a smaller, family-sized version. Follow the method as above, but halve the amounts of all ingredients except the chocolate. Use a 6-cup ovenproof dish and cook at 180C.

Chef Colin Masters, 1996

Chocolate almond meringue torte

"I remember my Mum cooking it to oohs and aahs from appreciative guests when I was in my teens ... it has stood the test of time and everyone who tries it asks for the recipe," says Janne Apelgren. "It's even better the next day, really chewy and gooey, but rarely survives long enough for anyone to find out."

2 egg whites
½ cup castor sugar
½ cup blanched almonds, chopped roughly, not too fine
grated chocolate or cocoa powder, to decorate
Filling
¾ cup semi-sweet chocolate pieces
2 tbsp hot water
½ tsp vanilla essence
1 cup thickened cream, whipped

Preheat oven to 135C.

Butter a 23cm pie plate, or place a circle of baking paper that size on an oven tray.

Beat egg whites stiffly and add the castor sugar gradually, beating well after each addition. Fold in the nuts. Spread the meringue on the tray or pie plate.

Bake on the middle shelf of the oven until delicately brown (60-75 minutes). Cool thoroughly. (The meringue can be made a day in advance of serving).

For the filling, melt chocolate thoroughly in a double saucepan. Add hot water and cook until thickened. Cool slightly. The mixture will become quite thick. Add the vanilla. Fold the whipped cream into the chocolate. Combine well, but don't beat. Pour into meringue and chill for two hours. Decorate with grated chocolate or cocoa powder.

Janne Apelgren, Epicure editor 1988-1989

Groggy dessert cake

If you love Baileys, you'll love this moist, wickedly alcoholic dessert cake.

150g unsalted butter
250g dark chocolate
165g castor sugar
3 eggs
1 cup ground almonds
1 cup Baileys Irish Cream liqueur
1½ cups plain flour
¼ cup Dutch cocoa

Preheat oven to 150C. Grease and line a 24cm springform cake tin.
   Melt butter in a saucepan. Add chocolate and stir over low heat until chocolate has melted and mixture is smooth. Remove from heat.
   Add sugar and stir to combine.
   Beat in eggs, one at a time, and mix until smooth and glossy.
   Stir in ground almonds.
   Add Baileys Irish Cream.
   Sift the flour and cocoa together and gradually add to mixture.
   Pour into the tin and bake for 45-50 minutes until a skewer comes out almost clean.
   Leave in cake tin for 10 minutes or so to cool, then turn out onto a wire rack.
   Serve dusted with cocoa or icing sugar.

Epicure stylist Caroline Velik

savoury153

Mexican pasta

This draws on two cuisines, combining a rich, sweet-savoury sauce inspired by the Mexican mole with one of the staples of Italian cooking.

400g dried papardelle pasta
olive oil
2-3 spring onions, finely sliced
5cm piece hot salami, finely sliced
800g tin diced tomatoes
75g dark chocolate (min 70 per cent cocoa), chopped
salt and pepper to taste
1 bunch fresh picked coriander leaves

Cook pasta in large pot of boiling salted water. When cooked, drain and set aside.

Heat oil in large frying pan. Add white parts of the spring onions to the pan, reserving the green tips for later. Fry onions and salami until caramelising.

Add the tomatoes and cook over medium heat to reduce slightly. Add chocolate pieces and stir through until melted and smooth.

Add salt and pepper to taste. Add coriander and green onion tips and allow to wilt.

Stir some of the sauce through the pasta, coating well, then top with the remaining sauce.

Don't add cheese.
Serves 4

Reader Richard Evans

Mole

This intense, dark Mexican sauce is one of the best-known examples of the happy marriage of chocolate and chilli. It goes well with chicken, duck or other poultry.

450g tin peeled tomatoes
2 tsp dried red chilli flakes
$\frac{1}{4}$ tsp garam masala
$\frac{1}{4}$ tsp cinnamon
$\frac{1}{4}$ tsp ground cloves
3-4 shallots or small onions, peeled and halved
2 garlic cloves, peeled and smashed
100g blanched almonds
50g seedless raisins
2 tbsp sesame seeds
1 tbsp butter
1 cup chicken stock
50g good dark chocolate, roughly chopped

Drain the tomatoes, reserving $\frac{1}{4}$ cup of the juice. Put the tomatoes, reserved juice, chilli, spices, shallots, garlic, almonds, raisins and sesame seeds into a food processor and blitz until smooth.

Melt the butter in a saucepan, add the mixture and cook, stirring continuously, for 10-15 minutes, then add chicken stock. Return almost to the boil and add the chocolate. Cook over moderate heat, stirring occasionally, for a further 10-15 minutes until it achieves a good sauce consistency and gloss. Serve over poultry.
Serves 4

Reader Michael Oliphant

Mole

Grilled pork with spicy chocolate sauce

Many overseas writers have contributed to Epicure. In one such article, a fascinating sweep through the long history of chocolate, American author/historian Charles Perry related the Aztec practice of enriching chocolate drinks with honey, herbs, spices, flowers, chillies and brightly coloured dyes. The Europeans who followed would add ground nuts, musk, ambergris, annatto or rosewater to their cocoa confections. Perry's own recipe seems almost tame in comparison – a spicy chocolate sauce that shows that savoury recipes, too, can be enhanced by chocolate.

1 pork tenderloin, about 700g

1 medium-sized red onion, cut into wedges

oil

salt, pepper

Chocolate-tomatillo sauce

3 dried red California chillies

¼ cup chicken stock

1 large onion, chopped

3 large cloves garlic, minced

3 jalapeno chillies, finely chopped

2 tbsp oil

450g tomatillos, papery husks removed, quartered

1 cup orange juice

25g bittersweet chocolate, chopped

¼ tspn hot red pepper, crushed

¼ cup coriander, chopped

For the sauce: toast the chillies in a hot dry skillet until soft. Remove the stems and seeds. In a blender, process the chillies with the stock to form a smooth paste. Set aside.

Saute the onion, garlic and jalapenos in oil until tender.

Stir in the tomatillos and orange juice. Bring to the boil. Reduce the heat and simmer, stirring occasionally, until the tomatillos are cooked and the sauce forms, 20-25 minutes. Stir in the reserved chilli paste and chocolate. Heat and stir just until chocolate melts.

Stir in crushed red pepper, salt and pepper to taste. Add coriander. Keep warm while preparing pork kebabs.

Cut tenderloin lengthwise into six strips. Pound lightly to flatten slightly. Thread on skewers with red onion wedges. Brush with oil.

Grill until onion begins to char and meat is done through. Season to taste with salt and pepper while grilling.

Spoon over 2 tablespoons chocolate-tomatillo sauce for each serving.

Serves 6

Note: Tinned tomatillos can be substituted if fresh ones are not available. Reduce the cooking time to approximately 10 minutes. Tinned tomatillos are available at specialist grocers that stock Mexican foods.

Writer Charles Perry, 1994

This recipe appears courtesy of the Los Angeles Times

"The fabulous thing about good-quality chocolate is that you can do everything with it or nothing at all, and the results are almost guaranteed to be popular! You can serve up plain ol' chunks of it, melt it, shave it, dip into it or flavour with it. Such a versatile ingredient. "

Miranda Sharp

Cervo in salmi (venison stew)

"There's something about home-made pappardelle – thin, broad, slippery, unevenly cut ribbons of egg-pasta – that really suits dark, rich meat sauces. A traditional Italian ragu seems right, and that's how I remember this venison at Florentino one winter lunch," says Epicure restaurant writer John Lethlean. "The meat has a flavour of its own after all that marinating, but it's the sauce that is memorable." The recipe is by Grossi Florentino's Guy Grossi, who generously agreed to its inclusion in this book. It also appears in his book, *My Italian Heart* (Lantern, 2005). There, he suggests cutting the meat finely to make a ragu, or larger to make a dish to serve with polenta.

2 kg boned venison shoulder (see note),
   cut into cubes
200ml olive oil
1 cup tomato paste
1 litre veal, chicken, beef or venison stock
1 tbsp Dutch cocoa
1 tbsp strawberry jam
1 tsp brandy
cooked polenta or pappardelle, to serve

Marinade
1 onion, diced
1 large carrot, diced
1 large stick celery, diced
2 cloves garlic, crushed
1 tsp fresh rosemary, chopped
1 tsp fresh sage, chopped
1 tsp fresh flat-leaf parsley, chopped
1 tsp juniper berries, crushed
pinch of freshly grated nutmeg
pinch of ground cumin
1 litre red wine
sea salt
black pepper, freshly ground

To make the marinade, combine all the ingredients in a large glass or ceramic dish. Add the venison, turning to coat. Cover and refrigerate overnight.

Next day, remove the meat from the marinade. Strain the marinade and reserve both the liquid and the vegetables.

Heat 50ml of the olive oil in a large, heavy-based pot. Add one third of the venison and brown on all sides. Remove from the pot and set aside. Repeat twice more to brown remaining meat.

Heat another 50ml of the olive oil in the pot, then add the reserved vegetables and saute for 3-4 minutes. Add the tomato paste and cook for 5 minutes, stirring continuously to prevent sticking. Return the venison to the pot and pour in the reserved marinade liquid and the stock. Mix well, then reduce the heat and simmer gently for 1 hour, stirring occasionally to prevent sticking.

Put the cocoa, jam and brandy in a bowl. Heat until the cocoa has dissolved, mixing well to avoid lumps. Add the cocoa mixture to the stew and mix well. Cook for a further 5 minutes, then taste a piece of the meat – it should be tender.

Serve immediately, accompanied by polenta or pappardelle.
Serves 6

Note: Venison can be obtained by most butchers if you give them a bit of notice.

John Lethlean, Epicure editor 2000-2001

Stuffed mulato chillies

"This has a wonderfully rich and exciting aroma," says Courtney Thackray. A complex, chocolate-spiked sauce combines with smoky chillies and a spicy pork stuffing in a Mexican-style dish for those who like a little adventure in their cooking. The sauce can also be used for a simpler meatball dish.

Stuffing
1 clove garlic, finely chopped
½ small onion, finely chopped
splash of olive oil
½ tsp cumin
1 tsp cinnamon
1 tsp paprika
½ tsp smoked paprika
½ tsp dried oregano
½ tsp allspice
400g pork mince
1 tbsp almond meal, lightly toasted
1 tbsp ground hazelnuts, lightly toasted
1 tbsp toasted pine nuts

1 tsp sugar
½ tsp salt
½ tsp ground black pepper
8 dried mulato chillies (for alternatives,
      see the variations listed below)
Sauce
1 tsp paprika
½ cup tomato pomodoro
1 tsp sugar
½ cup chicken stock
½ cup water
salt to taste
½ tsp cinnamon
50g good quality dark bitter chocolate, grated

Preheat oven to 220C.

Fry garlic and onion in olive oil until soft. Add herbs and spices and stir to combine. Turn off heat and allow to cool.

Combine pork mince, almond and hazelnut meal, pine nuts, sugar, salt and pepper. Add to cooled onion mix. Mix very well to combine. Refrigerate for at least 1 hour.

Cut a round into the stem end of each chilli and remove the stem and seeds. Be careful not to break the skin. Gently stuff the chillies with the pork mixture and arrange in a casserole dish. Ensure they are placed quite closely together to fit the casserole.

To make the sauce: in a large pan, heat the paprika gently for 20 seconds. Be careful not to burn it. Add the tomato and sugar and cook for 1 minute on a medium heat. Add chicken stock, water, salt to taste, cinnamon and grated chocolate and mix together to combine.

Pour mixture over chillies. The mixture should come most of the way up the sides of

the chillies. With the casserole lid on bake for 15 minutes. Turn down the oven to 170C and bake for a further 40 minutes with the lid ajar. Turn each chilli very carefully with a spoon once during the cooking process.

Serve with fragrant rice and an avocado-inclusive salad.
Serves 8 as an entree or 4 as a main course

Variations
1. Dried mulato chillies are available at some specialist food retailers. Dried ancho chillies can be substituted, but are not as aromatic.
2. Replace the pork mince with turkey mince and mix it with ½ tsp of salt, 2 tbsp of breadcrumbs and half a beaten egg along with other stuffing ingredients as instructed above. Roll the mixture into meatballs and immerse in the sauce. Cook as instructed above.

Reader Courtney Thackray

sweets, drinks + sauces165

English toffee

Forget the tooth-breaking toffees of childhood memory. This is completely different –
a gentler, nut-studded confection that not only freezes well but tastes oh-so-good straight
out of the freezer.

500g whole, skin-on raw almonds
500g unsalted European-style butter
1 tsp fleur de sel (or kosher salt) or
   ½ tsp table salt
2 cups white sugar
2 tsp vanilla essence
300g good quality bittersweet chocolate
   (e.g. Lindt)

Pulse the almonds three or four times in a food processor until they are broken into large chunks. Remove about half and set aside. Grind the remaining almonds into a coarse meal. Set aside. Melt butter with salt in a medium-sized saucepan over medium heat. Stir the sugar in slowly with a wooden spoon.

Continue cooking, stirring pretty constantly for about 15 minutes. The sugar will at first sink to the bottom of the pot. It will gradually melt and begin to incorporate into the butter. The mixture will turn from yellow to off-white and begin to look like taffy, gaining slightly in volume and turning slightly elastic. It will then gradually darken to tan, keeping a pearlescent appearance. When it turns tan, stir in the large chunks of almond and the vanilla, which will darken the toffee. Continue stirring until the almonds begin to toast and become very fragrant, about 5-10 minutes – your nose will tell you when it's ready. (If it begins to "sweat" a few beads of butter on the surface, take it off the heat.)

Stir it vigorously off the heat then pour into an ungreased nonstick 25cm x 38cm baking sheet and help it to settle into the corners of the pan.

Cut chocolate into chunks and melt over a double boiler. Spread half the chocolate over the surface of the cooling toffee with a pastry spatula. Cover with half the finely ground almonds. When cool enough to harden (about 20 minutes at room temperature), invert pan over another pan and bend it to loosen the toffee. (Don't worry if it cracks.) Spread the other side with melted chocolate and dust with the remaining ground almonds.

Place in refrigerator to harden thoroughly. Break into pieces and pack with any excess ground almonds into airtight containers or bags. Refrigerate or freeze until ready to serve.

Reader Vanessa Denney

"Scrumbo" honey fudge

This soft, sugary treat with a distinct honey note illustrates the fine tradition of recipe sharing. "This recipe was given to me many years ago by a young Irish neighbour, who swore this 'secret' recipe was passed on to him while in the US. Being Irish, he had a quirky way with words and it was always referred to as 'Scrumbo' fudge" says Judith Caine, who now passes it on again.

150g butter
500g sugar
2 tbsp honey
115g dark chocolate
115ml milk
few drops vanilla essence

Grease a 15cm square tray.

Place all ingredients except vanilla into a double boiler over medium heat, stirring until sugar is dissolved. Cook until mixture makes a soft ball when dropped in a saucer of cold water (118C on candy thermometer). Remove from heat, add vanilla and beat well until mixture becomes thick and glossy. Pour quickly into the tray and allow to set, marking into squares while still warm.

Reader Judith Caine

Sultana and nut fudge

A smooth, caramel/chocolate fudge studded with fruit and nuts, this is easy to make and very easy to eat.

3 cups milk chocolate chips
395g tin condensed milk
¼ cup butter
handful sultanas
handful crushed nuts

Place chocolate, condensed milk and butter in a large bowl. Microwave at medium until chocolate chips have melted (2-5 minutes). Stir regularly during cooking. Add sultanas and nuts, pour into a container (20cm x 20cm) lined with cling wrap and refrigerate.

Variations: Use diced preserved ginger instead of the fruit and nuts, or make a plain fudge flavoured with a few drops of peppermint oil.

Reader Glynis Smalley

Milky fudge

A super-sweet and slightly gooey fudge for those who like white chocolate.

550g white chocolate
395g tin condensed milk
2 tsp vanilla essence

Line a 20cm square tin with baking paper. Melt chocolate and condensed milk in microwave or in a double-boiler. Add vanilla and mix well. Spread mixture in tin and place in fridge to set. When set, cut into squares.

Variation: Add pistachios, cranberries or other fruit and nuts.
Note: The "goo factor" in this fudge depends on the ratio of chocolate to condensed milk. If you want a softer fudge (which would also make an indulgent icing for cupcakes, if used before it starts setting), reduce the amount of white chocolate.

Reader Michael Oliphant

Hot chocolate

This is not the most difficult recipe in the world, but everyone needs to know how to make hot chocolate (or direct someone else to the page so they can do it whilst you are curled up on the couch in your thick socks and daggy dressing gown).

½ cup Dutch cocoa powder or good quality drinking chocolate
5 tbsp boiling water
3-4 tbsp castor sugar (to taste)
600ml full-cream milk
16-20 marshmallows
100g good quality dark chocolate, broken into chunks

Blend cocoa powder with boiling water to a smooth paste. Add sugar to sweeten.

Pour two tablespoons of this chocolate mix into each cup.

Heat milk in a small saucepan. Do not boil! Remove from heat.

Pour hot milk into cups and stir well. Top each cup with 4-5 marshmallows and allow them to melt into the hot chocolatey drink.

Serve with chunks of chocolate, which can be added to each mug to melt slowly and gloriously away in the bottom, so that you finish with an intense molten chocolate hit!
Serves 4

Epicure stylist Caroline Velik

Cheat's truffles

"Forget all the usual fiddling about – these are a breeze to make," says Barbara McNeill. They are indeed easy, and incredibly rich. The mixture would also make an indulgent cake icing.

500g chocolate
about 2 tsp Kahlua
250g mascarpone cheese
about ¾ cup Dutch cocoa

Melt the chocolate. Add a small slosh of Kahlua, or other liqueur (chocolate or coffee-flavoured ones are best), and blend well. Remove from heat, wait until it is cool enough to put your index finger in without burning, then stir in the mascarpone. Pop in the fridge to let it firm up (about 30 minutes). You want it firm, but still malleable.

To shape the truffles, you can either use a melon baller for neat truffles, or make them look more artistically truffly by using a teaspoon. Roll in cocoa in a shallow tray to prevent them sticking.
Makes about 44 truffles

Variations: After the liqueur, you can add a handful of chopped macadamias, or smashed up almond toffee.

Reader Barbara McNeill

Praline truffles

Sometimes one's mood demands a super-rich truffle – and sometimes it doesn't. This is the perfect not-too-sweet truffle, with a wonderful crunch and flavour from the crushed praline.

125g castor sugar
¼ cup water
125g slivered almonds
60ml cream
300g good quality chocolate, finely chopped
½-¾ cup cocoa, for dusting

For the praline, combine sugar and water and stir over a low heat until sugar dissolves. Increase heat and boil until golden in colour. Stir in almonds and pour onto an oiled baking tray. Cool until hard then grind with a mortar and pestle (or place in a plastic bag on a chopping block and smash with a rolling pin).

Heat cream in heavy based saucepan until it just reaches boiling point. Put chocolate into cream and stir, using a plastic spoon. Stir gently until smooth. Mix in 3-4 tablespoons of praline. Place in fridge for about one hour, to firm.

Line a baking tray with baking paper.
Roll about ¾ teaspoon of chocolate mixture into a ball using fingertips. Roll in cocoa. Place on prepared tray. Return to fridge to firm. Repeat with remaining mixture.
Serve with espresso coffee.
Makes about 48

Reader Lindis Krejus

Double truffles

These two-tone truffles make a lovely gift (and can be prepared ahead and stored in the fridge or freezer).

White centre
1 tbsp light corn syrup
½ cup thickened cream
300g white chocolate, grated

Chocolate coating
90g unsalted butter
385g dark chocolate
⅓ cup thickened cream
4 tbsp brandy or Grand Marnier
cocoa, to coat truffles

For the white centre: put the corn syrup and cream into a saucepan. Bring to the boil.

Immediately add the white chocolate; shake and swirl so that the chocolate is covered with the cream. Put a lid on the pan and allow it to rest for about 3 minutes. The white chocolate should melt. If it doesn't, warm the pan carefully again (for example, standing in a pan of hot water).

Put into a lightly oiled or buttered bowl and leave to cool, then chill. When firm enough to handle, form into 12 balls. Freeze until firm.

For the chocolate coating: melt the butter over low heat, and when bubbling gently on the edges, add dark chocolate and immediately remove from heat. Stir until smooth. Add cream and Grand Marnier and mix. Chill until firm.

Divide into 12 portions and return to refrigerator.

Sift the cocoa onto a plate ready for rolling the truffles.

Take out one coating portion at a time so that they remain cold and easier to handle.

Form each into a ball, then flatten out. Wrap this section around the white centre, smoothing it with your hands to make a roundish shape with slightly uneven surfaces.

Roll the ball in the cocoa.

Freeze again until firm.

Repeat with remaining portions.

The truffles can be stored in the freezer for up to 12 weeks (or up to 10 days in the refrigerator).

To serve, these can be cut in quarters, then returned to the refrigerator until needed (cut with a knife dipped in boiling water).

Columnist Beverley Sutherland Smith, 1994

Chocolate caramel fudge

Kim Broadfoot – then Kim Baxter – shared her recipe for this wickedly rich treat in Epicure's Ask The Chef column in 1996, when she was the chef and co-owner of a Melbourne cafe called Fresh.

190g unsalted butter
150g white marshmallows
375ml tin evaporated milk
400g castor sugar
275g milk chocolate
1½ tsp vanilla essence
Ganache topping
150ml thickened cream
125g unsalted butter
200g milk chocolate

Lightly grease a shallow 15cm x 20cm tray.

Combine butter, marshmallows, evaporated milk and castor sugar in a pot. Stir over a low heat until the sugar and marshmallows have dissolved. Bring to the boil for about 10 minutes, stirring continuously to make sure the fudge does not burn on the bottom or sides. (The constant stirring is crucial to success with this recipe.)

When it has turned a caramel colour, remove from the heat.

Allow to cool slightly, then add chocolate and vanilla. Mix well, stirring until the chocolate has melted. Pour into the prepared tin and allow to cool in the fridge.

Combine ganache ingredients in a heavy-based pot. Stir over a low heat until the butter and chocolate melt and the mixture binds together. Pour over the fudge and allow to set before cutting. (This can be set in the fridge, but it might take the shine off the ganache.)

Store in the fridge.

Kim Broadfoot, 1996

Cheat Christmas chocolate clusters

Since it began in 2001, Miranda Sharp's "Cheat" column in Epicure has shared many easy, delicious recipes with appreciative readers, including this seasonal treat.

2 cups sugar
1 cup water
325g roasted unsalted nuts (I like a hazelnut
   and almond combo)
200g couverture chocolate

Make a toffee by dissolving sugar in water, bringing to the boil and gradually allowing it to thicken and caramelise, which will take about 15 minutes. Do not stir once dissolved. When the toffee is taking on a golden (but not dark!) colour, remove from the heat and stir in nuts. Pour this molten mix onto a greased baking tray with sides about 2-3cm high and allow it to start cooling.

Test the mix as it cools and when it can be handled, pick up toffee/nut clusters comprising about three nuts and press together into imperfect balls. Allow to harden. You'll only have about 15 minutes between the mix being too hot and too hard so work quickly, and give up when you can't separate them any more. The remaining mix can cool as one block and be broken up inside a plastic bag tapped with a mallet or hammer later.

Melt chocolate gently in a small bowl over simmering water or in a microwave.

Dip toffee/nut clusters completely and remove with a fork, cool and allow to solidify on non-stick paper in the fridge.

Store in the fridge.

Columnist Miranda Sharp, 2002

Chocolate sauce

Helen Rouse found this recipe more than 20 years ago, when she bought a copy of the Port Fairy Kindergarten Recipe Book during a Christmas holiday. The Port Fairy Preschool kindly allowed us to republish it here. It makes a smooth, not-too-thick sauce good for pouring over ice-cream, brownies or puddings.

¾ cup sugar
3 tbsp cocoa
1 cup water
2 tbsp golden syrup
1 tbsp cornflour
1 tsp butter
1 tsp vanilla essence

Mix together sugar, cocoa and ½ cup of water in a small saucepan. Add golden syrup and heat. When just boiling, add cornflour mixed with the other ½ cup of water. Lastly, add butter and vanilla. Cook, stirring, for a few minutes until mixture thickens slightly.
Makes approx 375ml

Reader Helen Rouse

Chocolate icing

225g icing sugar
1 heaped tbsp cocoa
1 tbsp melted butter
1 tsp vanilla essence (optional)
warm water

Sift icing sugar and cocoa. Mix in butter, vanilla and enough water to give a spreadable consistency. Beat until smooth.

Kylie Walker, Epicure editor

Chocolate ganache

1 cup thickened cream
200g dark cooking chocolate, chopped
1 tsp unsalted butter

Heat cream in a saucepan over low heat. Add chocolate and mix until it is melted. Add butter and stir to combine. Remove from heat.

 Alternatively, melt chocolate in microwave with cream for approximately 2 minutes on medium. Remove from microwave and stir. Repeat until melted and combined.

 Ganache can be used whilst it is quite runny or you can leave it to thicken before icing the cake.

Variation: For white chocolate ganache substitute white chocolate in the recipe above.

Epicure stylist Caroline Velik

"Chocolate … mmm … my favourite thing is going to bed with a hot chocolate made with melted Valrhona and a splash of rum – so delicious! It evokes childhood memories of eating chocolate from the advent calendar at Christmas … of walking into the house and inhaling the smell of a chocolate cake baking

Kentucky bourbon candies

"This is an old family recipe handed down to me by my grandmother, who made them as gifts each Christmas," says Candy Maughan. Sweet, alcohol-dosed icing is offset by salty nuts, all dipped in chocolate.

250g icing sugar
25g soft butter
⅓ cup good bourbon
60 salted pecan halves
Coating
250g semi-sweet chocolate
1 tbsp butter

Mix the first three ingredients until dough-like. Cover and refrigerate at least 3 hours.
   Make into small balls and sandwich between 2 salted pecan halves; chill again.
   Melt coating ingredients in a double boiler and mix. Dip candies in chocolate and allow to set. Store in fridge.

Variations: Raw, unsalted pecans could be used instead of salted nuts. Candy's grandmother also made a version using creme de menthe in the filling and white chocolate in the coating mixture.
Note: The original included paraffin in the coating for shine. We have omitted it as the recipe works without it and some people are allergic to it.

Reader Candy Maughan

Chocolate faery

15ml absinthe
30ml chocolate schnapps (or another chocolate liqueur)

Pour into a decorative glass and add ice if desired.

Reader Vicky Vladic

Orange Cointreau syrup

A citrussy, slightly sweet sauce to serve over ice-cream or poached fruit.

2 oranges, zest peeled and julienned and the juice
   placed through a fine sieve
150g castor sugar
1 vanilla bean, split in half lengthways
100ml water
60ml Cointreau

Blanch the zest and refresh in ice water three times. You can use the same blanching water each time and you only need to submerge the zest for 20 seconds each time.
   In another pot mix together the orange juice, sugar, vanilla bean, water and the drained zest. Reduce by half then add cointreau last and just bring to the boil. Remove from heat. Remove vanilla bean.

Reader Sonia Anthony

Chocolate faery

Adults-only rocky road

"This road is not so much rocky as paved with chocolate," says
Nigel Brew of his liqueur-laced version of this traditional treat.

250g packet of mixed pink/white marshmallows
100g real glace cherries
165g packet of Maltesers
2-3 tbsp Grand Marnier
250g dark cooking chocolate
100g copha

Line a shallow lamington tin with baking paper.
    Halve marshmallows and cherries and place in a bowl with Maltesers.
Sprinkle Grand Marnier over the contents of the bowl while mixing with
a spoon to evenly distribute (save some to mix into the melted
chocolate as well for an even richer taste, if desired).
    Melt chocolate and copha together.
    Pour melted chocolate mixture over the other ingredients and mix
well. Pour/scoop mixture into tin and refrigerate until set. Cut to
desired size.
Makes about 15 snack-sized squares

Reader Nigel Brew

"Adult" hedgehog

A boozy version of the classic.

150g pitted prunes, chopped
spirit or liqueur such as brandy, Drambuie, Grand Marnier
150g Granita biscuits (or similar)
150g Gingernut biscuits (or similar)
250g dark couverture chocolate
150g butter
140g roasted hazelnuts, roughly chopped
150ml cream, whipped

Soak prunes overnight in enough grog to just cover.

Roughly crush biscuits, leaving plenty of small pieces for texture.

Melt chocolate and butter in bowl over simmering water, cool a little then combine with biscuits, hazelnuts and prunes, with their liquid. Fold cream through and press into a paper-lined springform tin.

Cover and refrigerate until firm. Serve in thin slices sprinkled with cocoa.

Columnist Miranda Sharp, 2003

After-dinner brownies

Packed with sweet glacé fruit and studded with white and milk chocolate chips, this rich after-dinner treat was the happy result of a kitchen experiment. "I was intending to make tiny Florentines for a dinner party and ran out of time. Brownies are so quick and easy, and I had the glacé fruit to hand, so I made these instead," explains Chris Sackville.

60g glacé fruit
1 tbsp of rum or liqueur
125g unsalted butter
150g dark chocolate
½ cup castor sugar
2 eggs, lightly beaten
1¼ cups plain flour, sifted
150g white chocolate chopped
100g milk chocolate, chopped

Chop the fruit and soak in rum for an hour or so.

Preheat oven to 180C. Grease and line base and sides of a 20cm square pan.

Melt butter and dark chocolate over simmering water. Cool slightly. Stir in sugar, lightly beaten eggs and glacé fruit mixture. Fold in sifted flour, then fold in white and milk chocolate.

Spread in prepared pan and bake in oven for about 35 minutes or until firm to touch. Cool in pan before removing. Cut into small squares.

Variations: Glacé pineapple and cherries with rum is good, as is home-made glacé orange peel with orange liqueur.

Reader Chris Sackville

After-dinner brownies

STEPHANIE ALEXANDER

Stephanie Alexander has owned and operated restaurants in Melbourne for more than 30 years. She has written 11 books, including the award-winning Australian classic *The Cooks Companion*, first published in 1996 with a revised and expanded edition published in 2004. She is chair of The Stephanie Alexander Kitchen Garden Foundation, established in 2004, which is working to expand the successful project operating at Melbourne's Collingwood College, so that more young children can learn about growing, harvesting, preparing and sharing good food. She has written for *The Age* on many topics and currently writes a fortnightly food column in Epicure.

JILL DUPLEIX

Jill Dupleix was born on a sheep farm in Victoria, and has lived and cooked in Melbourne, Sydney and London. She has been writing recipes for Epicure since 1994, and has published 13 cookbooks, the latest being *Good Cooking: The New Essentials*. She was Epicure's weekly food columnist from 1996 to 2000.

BRIGITTE HAFNER

Brigitte Hafner has loved cooking since she was old enough to hang off her mother's kitchen bench, watching and sneaking tastes of whatever she was making. She has since worked alongside Kylie Kwong, Neil Perry, Jacques Reymond, Greg Malouf and Stefano de Pieri. She owns and runs the Gertrude Street Enoteca in Fitzroy, Melbourne, where she is honing her wine knowledge, writing about food and enjoying her new kitchen. She has contributed to Epicure since 2004.

DONNA HAY

Donna Hay began her career as a freelance food writer and stylist when she was 19. Donna's work focused on basic ingredients, simply prepared and beautifully presented – a hallmark of her work that evolved further when she became the food director of *marie claire Australia*. In November 2001 Donna launched the bi-monthly *donna hay magazine*, which rapidly became

Australia's fastest growing food title. She has also published nine cookbooks. Donna contributed a weekly food column to Epicure in 2001.

LUKE MANGAN

Inspired by the hearty, Irish family cooking of his childhood in the outer Melbourne suburbs, chef Luke Mangan has made a career as a chef and consultant. In his early years he worked with, among others, Hermann Schneider at Two Faces in Melbourne and at the three-Michelin-star Waterside Inn in Berkshire, England under chef Michel Roux. He opened his first restaurant, Salt, in Sydney in 1993. Awards, more restaurants and several overseas consultancies followed. He has also written three cookbooks. Luke was Epicure's weekly food columnist from 2001 to 2004.

MIRANDA SHARP

Miranda Sharp ran a successful catering company called Black Tie for many years before making a foray into the world of food writing. She now writes a popular recipe column, called Cheat, for Epicure. She is also heavily involved in the community farmers' market movement, and was one of the driving forces behind the establishment of the very successful Collingwood Children's Farm monthly market.

BEVERLEY SUTHERLAND SMITH

An enthusiastic and passionate cook "from the moment she put a pan on the stove", Beverley Sutherland Smith turned her hobby of cooking into a vocation. Her cooking school, opened in 1967, was one of the first such schools in Melbourne and is still operating. She began writing for the *The Age* in 1977, and was Epicure's weekly cooking columnist from 1986 to 1996. She has written for magazines including *Gourmet* (now *Gourmet Traveller*) and *New Idea*, and has published 27 books.

In addition, we thank all of the chefs, readers and others who have generously contributed to Epicure's pages over the years and to this book.